121 Ways
Jesus Was There for Me

MY FAITH BECAME UNSHAKABLE THROUGHOUT MY MOM'S ALCOHOLISM

Rachel,

Jesus is there for you!

JoAnn Place

JoAnn Place

ISBN 979-8-88943-432-0 (paperback)
ISBN 979-8-88943-433-7 (digital)

Christian Faith Publishing
832 Park Avenue
Meadville, PA 16335
www.christianfaithpublishing.com

All biblical citations were taken from the English Standard Version of the Holy Bible unless indicated otherwise.

Printed in the United States of America

INTRODUCTION

Easter weekend 2022, I felt a very strong call to action from God. During the service at church, four personal testimonies were shared, and I was brought to tears with the request God put on my heart. God works in mysterious ways, and for the rest of that resurrection day, I couldn't stop thinking about his calling to write a book that could help someone. I kept thinking that I didn't know how to write a book. I'd never even thought about writing a book. But as I was trying to resist, God kept calling me to write about how Jesus was there for me.

In my past, I've been in really dark places in my mind and felt emotional pain that led me to thoughts about how to end it because I didn't think I could live another day bearing the pain. This came from my mom's alcoholism and the way the alcoholic version of my mom treated me and the dysfunction it brought to our family. Without Jesus, I wouldn't be here today enjoying the multitude of blessings given to me.

As I was thinking about how to go about writing, I decided I could do it in a document daily and then post it. I hoped that maybe it would help someone sooner than if I would wait until it's published. I decided to write one day at a time because AA and Al-Anon focus on living one day at a time. And for me, books that are read one day at a time make it easier to digest the content. I decided that each day, I'd write an entry about how Jesus was there for me and share a Bible verse.

I'd need to trust God to work through me to make the words flow. I didn't feel like I could write every day and had no idea how long it would take. My last attempt to resist was to ask my husband, Nate, if he thought it was a good idea. I had made up my mind that his answer would be my final decision, fully assuming he would probably say it wasn't a good idea. Without hesitation, he said, "Absolutely, you should."

Everyone has their share of struggles and pain in this imperfect world. I once learned that our greatest pain can be transformed into our greatest purpose. I pray this book will give people the hope and strength that can only come from Jesus.

Jesus was and is always there for me whether I realize it or not. He's there for you too. My intent is to give God all the glory, not me. I've tried to be raw and real. I encourage you to do your own writing along with reading mine. In a world filled with so much evil, we need to keep our focus on Jesus. He died for our sins, and if we believe in him, we are freely given eternal life in heaven with him instead of constant torment, burning in the eternal fires of hell with the devil.

"Rejoice in hope, be patient in tribulation, be constant in prayer" (Romans 12:12).

1

Prior to age twelve, my parents did an incredible job of raising my brother and me. I'm so grateful for the strong foundation I have as a result. My parents both worked in the Twin Cities and also raised crops on our farm. My mom worked day shift, and my dad worked afternoon shift. We went to church every Sunday, and my mom had taught Sunday school. We prayed and hugged before bed each night. And my parents loved to go dancing together on Saturday nights. As a family, we worked hard and played hard. I feel bad my brother only had eight of those good years. He's four years younger than me and doesn't remember much of the good years.

Maybe I was oblivious, or maybe it happened that quickly, but when I was twelve, everything changed. My mom stopped coming home after work. My parents would argue when my dad got home from work around 12:30 a.m. My mom would return shortly before then. My brother and I would be home alone together most weeknights.

On February 5, 1978, in Mr. Newville's Sunday school class, I accepted God's gift of eternal life. How do I know this? I still have the Bible I was given in Sunday school where I had written it down. I remember it vividly. Mr. Newville explained to us the importance of believing in Jesus, that he died for the forgiveness of our sins, and we need to accept God's gift—freely given, not earned. He prepped us with many verses in the Bible and let each of us decide when we were ready. It felt weird and uncomfortable, a public proclamation of faith among my classmates and teacher.

I took it seriously, studied the scripture, and didn't want to be the first one. Strange that this same message is repeated in so many different books of the Bible written by different people. I believe the Holy Spirit worked in me. In the presence of my class and teacher, I accepted God's gift of eternal life. My relationship with Jesus was locked in. Jesus was there for me. I had no idea how much I would need it in the coming years. I thank God for everyone he put in my life to help me build my faith and relationship with Jesus.

> No, in all these things we are more than conquerors through him who loved us. For I am sure that neither death nor life, nor angels nor rulers, nor things present nor things to come, nor powers, nor height nor depth, nor anything else in all creation, will be able to separate us from the love of God in Christ Jesus our Lord. (Romans 8:37–39)

2

For most, I think alcoholism sneaks in over time. Even the alcoholic doesn't realize it's getting a grip on them. I learned later that my mom's alcoholism probably started when she and her coworkers had drinks together over lunch. And, yes, they'd go back to work after lunch. That was back when you could smoke at your desk as well. As it was starting, she'd be home with us after work, and we didn't realize anything was happening. I really don't think she did either.

Then she started going to the bar after she made us dinner, or she drank beer on nights she stayed home. I was young enough that I didn't realize a problem was developing and had not heard of alcoholism at that point. But I started hating the sound of a can opening.

When my dad learned my brother and I were left alone while she was at the bar, he arranged with our friends who lived across the road that we could call them or go there to sleep when we were afraid. Their kids were the same ages as my brother and I, and we were all like one big family already, having grown up together.

Jesus was there for me. He gave me enough common sense to not do anything too stupid or careless, and he put people in our lives we could count on to help. We had the gift of this wonderful family right across the road who would welcome us in, no matter what time of the night. Although my dad was worried about what was happening with Mom and us, he could rest easy knowing we would be okay when Mom was at the bar and he was an hour away at work.

I wonder how many times I called our neighbor to ask questions about probably pretty basic things. Trying to take care of myself and my younger brother didn't come intuitively to me. Sometimes I would feel so afraid my brother and I would just run down the driveway to stay at the neighbors.

Just a few years ago, I was showing another friend's mom how I had decorated birthday cakes for my grandkids. She was the one who taught me how. I always admired her homemaking skills, and I often called her for help too. She loved the cakes and that I was still decorating them. She asked me, "Do you also remember how to wash clothes?" She said it in a lighthearted way, but I had to ask her what she was talking about. She said, "Don't you remember the time you called me and you were crying because you and your brother didn't have clean clothes to wear and you didn't know how to run the washing machine?"

Wow, no, I didn't remember that.

"For if they fall, one will lift up his fellow. But woe to him who is alone when he falls and has not another to lift him up!" (Ecclesiastes 4:10).

3

Don't get me wrong, our family continued to do fun things together and do what families do. But it was different. There was this sort of secret in our family that only we, our helpers, and maybe people at the bar knew about. And my mom usually had a can of beer in her hand, although this isn't uncommon in Wisconsin as I guess we're kind of known for our drinking.

It's amazing to me how families appear to roll along in life "as usual" while a loved one's alcoholism progresses. There are millions of families doing this right now at this moment. We never know what a person is going through, and I feel it is so important to give people grace. Maybe their behavior or response is driven by a pain they're carrying but never expose to anyone.

My parents still went to work, my brother and I went to school, we continued to work on our farm, we went to church every week, and we visited Grandma and Grandpa on Sundays. We had friends over and went to friends' houses. I would guess most people didn't know our secret, and I don't think we wanted anyone to know.

My mom's alcoholism progressed into the mean drunk stages. This resulted in nightly arguments between my parents. When Mom was drunk, she was a totally different person, someone we didn't even recognize. My dad would get home from work around 12:30 a.m.

and call her out for being drunk again, or she would just pick a fight with him. Although I was the only one who slept upstairs, I would wake up and lie there listening until the argument ended. I'm sure my brother did too. It wasn't really something easy to sleep through. This went on for years.

I remember lying there, thinking, *What is happening to our family? Why does she think she needs to drink all the time? I need to get some sleep. What can I do to fix this? I just want this to stop.* My heart would race, and I'd get all riled up. When the argument ended, I couldn't settle down to fall asleep again. But Jesus was there for me. I folded my hands and prayed to him until I fell asleep. I imagined one of my hands was his holding mine. I found peace and rest.

Manipulation is a skill that apparently comes as a bonus with alcoholism. A manipulative mean drunk will say and do really hurtful things. Looking back, my mom was now in the grip of alcoholism, no longer able to be herself. And my poor dad was trying to defend himself and help her, not realizing my mom was incapable of reasoning in that state. It must have been so devastating for him to see his beautiful loving wife behaving that way. I know it was very difficult to hear.

"In peace I will both lie down and sleep; for you alone, O Lord, make me dwell in safety" (Psalm 4:8).

4

Given my dad's efforts to try to help Mom see that alcohol was taking over her weren't working, I thought I would give it a go. *Maybe she'll listen to me.* I stayed awake until she came home from the bar to talk with her. That triggered her to lash out at me. I just don't know why I would think that trying to talk with her while she was drunk would be a good idea. I guess I didn't want to bring it up on a day when she wasn't drunk because I wanted the nice times together to be nice. I don't know how to explain it, but when you love someone so much and you're watching their life spiral out of control, you just want to keep trying to help them, thinking someday they'll understand what you're saying.

So now, as a teenager, I subjected myself to repeated verbal abuse from my own mother. Here's a sampling of what I was told. "It's all your fault this is happening." "I wouldn't drink if it wasn't for you." "Your life is so easy, you have no idea." "It must be nice being so thin and tan. I was never your size, and my skin burns." "You're just a whore."

I didn't even know what that meant, but when I found out what it was, I definitely wasn't that. I can't adequately describe in words the way I felt. Her words sucked the life out of me and made me question if I was a good person or not, especially the way she said these things to me. *Why is she so angry and screaming at me? Maybe this is my fault. I mean, she is my mom, older and wiser than me.*

I would say, "Mom, you're so beautiful and such a wonderful person. Why are you doing this? We want you to be home with us. We miss you. We love you and always will. I'm praying for you, asking God to please help you stop drinking so much."

There was one night, after many, that we were still screaming at each other when my dad got home from work. I was so upset, shaking, exhausted, going out of my mind, feeling like I just wanted to run away, thinking that maybe my whole family would just be better off without me.

My dad walked in, took one look at me, walked over, and wrapped me in his arms. I literally collapsed with him holding me, so he gently sat both of us down onto the floor where I would have fallen otherwise. I sobbed uncontrollably. Jesus was there for me. Not only did I feel relief and safety in my daddy's arms, I could feel Jesus was there with all of us. I imagine Jesus was crying (like I am right now writing this) because the free will we're all given wasn't being used for what he'd want. Fully in the grip of alcoholism, Mom's will was to keep drinking too much, even though she had to have seen it was hurtful. My dad's and my will was to keep arguing with her, even though it wasn't helping anything.

"The Lord is near to the brokenhearted and saves the crushed in spirit" (Psalm 34:18).

5

To help you understand what we were losing, I want to tell you about my mom. She was the kindest, most compassionate, caring, generous, loving, faithful, fun, strongest, most beautiful woman I've ever met.

She grew up in Glenwood City, the youngest of seven surviving children, born in 1941, and twenty years younger than her oldest sibling. Their family was poor like most at that time, even though Grandpa worked very hard. He had only gone to school through third grade but was smart as a whip.

Mom wore hand-me-downs, and Grandma was very strict. Mom made the cheerleading team and cheered, but Grandma wouldn't let her go to the bowling alley after games. She graduated salutatorian of her class and had many friends.

My mom and dad met while in high school, even though my dad lived in Spring Valley. They went on a Luther League trip to Montana and met while on the trip. Someone had anonymously donated the money for my mom to go; otherwise, she couldn't have afforded it. Mom and Dad must have fallen in love at first sight because after my dad came home from serving in the army in Germany years later, he asked her out, and they were married shortly after.

After graduation, my mom moved to the big city of St. Paul to work in an office. She and her girlfriend rented a place there. She told me of a time when she was walking home and was robbed at knifepoint. She said she fainted from fear, and the robber ran away as she really had nothing for him to rob.

Mom would drive to Glenwood City on weekends to take Grandma and Grandpa to visit other relatives. She did so much for others and rarely anything for herself. The lesson to take away from this is that self-care is important. If we give, give, give and never fill our cups back up, it costs us our ability to care for others because we didn't take care of ourselves. Much later, I found out—I believe from what she told me—that drinking became the thing she did for herself.

As a wife and mother, she did so much for us. She loved us deeply, and we felt her love was a special kind of love. She worked so hard, commuting to work and working on our farm and taking care of us. My dad too. She was a great cook and baker, gardener, card player, Sunday school teacher, volunteer at church, helper of neighbors. Our parents made going to church and Sunday school a priority and taught us about Jesus and the importance of a relation-ship with him. A sign with praying hands hung in our home. It said "A family that prays together stays together." We prayed together.

Before alcoholism crept in, we had what I would call the best childhood ever. Mom and Dad provided everything we needed, and I don't remember a single want that went unfulfilled. We hosted Luther League sliding parties at our farm. We also hosted birthday parties and family and neighborhood get-togethers. Our neighbor-hood (our mile stretch of road) had five other kids in two families that my brother and I played with, and our church was at the end of our road. We were blessed with the best of everything.

This was my mom and how I'll always remember her. Jesus was there for me. Mom's love for everyone was always still there, and our love for her was and always will be too.

"And above all these put on love, which binds everything together in perfect harmony" (Colossians 3:14).

6

When your loved one is an alcoholic, it almost feels like they're two different people. We had my mom we knew and loved. And we had the alcoholic we didn't recognize. Most times, it was difficult to separate the two. My mom was the strongest woman I knew. How could alcoholism possibly be powerful enough to overcome her? So is it her doing and saying hurtful things? How do I know? Why is she doing what she does? Why won't God make it stop? Why won't God heal her and our family?

Please know and remember throughout this book that the wonderful mom we knew and loved was still there, and we continued to enjoy some great times with her. I feel God is calling me to share the personal pain and struggles because those are the things rarely known by others, not often shared by people who experience them, even though there are millions who have been on this journey. The progression of alcoholism seems to be very predictable. Some are able to stop drinking, and others are not. I don't know why. They say people need to hit rock bottom, and perhaps the actual bottom is different for each alcoholic.

According to the NIH National Institute on Alcohol Abuse and Alcoholism, 14.5 million people ages twelve and over had alcohol use disorder (AUD) in 2019, with 414,000 aged twelve to seventeen. Approximately 10.5 percent (7.5 million) of US children aged seventeen and younger live with a parent with AUD, according to a 2017 report. Alcohol is the third-leading preventable cause of death in the United States. The first is tobacco, and the second is poor diet and physical inactivity.

When I was overwhelmed with pain, it's pretty crazy the different ways I thought of to escape it all. One of the craziest was waiting and hoping the UFOs would come get me. True story. In 1973, the nearby town of Elmwood, Wisconsin, started having UFO sightings reported. In 1978, they started the UFO Days, which is still celebrated annually the weekend of or near my birthday. I would literally sit by my upstairs bedroom window, watching and waiting for a UFO. There were stories and even a movie about alien abduction.

Considering the horrible things the stories said were done to the people abducted, I still concluded I probably deserved it and that everyone would be better off without me. I didn't want my family or me to continue to deal with this pain, and I kept hearing from my mom that I was the one to blame for it. So it would be best for the aliens to just come and take me away.

I was ready. I was so tired, being up late, listening to arguments between my parents or arguing with Mom myself and still getting up early to go to school or to work on the farm. With my brother and I being alone at night, I had to take on responsibilities because there was no other option. The aliens never came for me. Jesus was there for me. Every day, I found hope and strength from him. Every day, I prayed for him to please help us. Every night, I prayed so I could find the peace to fall asleep. Every day, I just kept keeping on.

"May the Lord give strength to his people! May the Lord bless his people with peace!" (Psalm 29:11).

7

Jesus was there for me. When I was twelve, a young mother with a girl who was two and a boy who was one called me out of the blue. She was wondering if I would be willing to babysit while she went to work three days a week after the school year ended for me. I asked my parents, and they agreed that I could. I didn't know them, but they lived only a couple of miles away, and she would pick me up and bring me back home.

This family made a huge difference in my life that I doubt they'll ever fully understand, and I'm forever grateful. The young father worked on the family farm, and they were still in the process of building a new beautiful home on the farm property. My job was to take care of the kids and make lunch for him. To this day, we laugh about how most days we had macaroni and cheese and hot dogs for lunch. I also voluntarily cleaned their house and did their laundry which was a treat for them that I didn't understand fully until I was a young mother. I loved to drink their milk fresh from the barn, cream on top. I had grown up drinking milk fresh from the bulk tank when our family still milked cows.

As I got to know them better, I learned he had an alcoholic father. Over lunch, we would have long conversations, and I finally knew someone who had a parent who was an alcoholic and could fully understand what I was going through. I continued to babysit for them every summer for six years and on weekend nights when they would go out together too. They welcomed a third child, another girl, so I took care of their three kids for most of those years.

They gave me birthday gifts. I believe it was the first gift, a sign with the Serenity Prayer, one of the most important gifts I have ever received. I memorized the Serenity Prayer and have prayed it countless times through the years. "God, grant me the serenity to accept the things I cannot change, courage to change the things I can, and the wisdom to know the difference." Amen to that!

I was becoming a control freak because there were very few things I had control over. It was and still is a lifelong lesson to learn that we can't control other people. God gave us all free will and chose not to control us. Instead, he gave his only Son to show us how to live, and then he died a horrific death so our sins can be forgiven if we believe and accept the gift of eternal life. We can only control ourselves and how we react to what happens to us or is said to us. And it's really important to know the difference between what we can control and what we cannot. Loving an alcoholic and dealing with their expert level of manipulation can literally make you crazy, so angry, and so hurt. Yet you keep going back for more because you so desperately want to try to change them, help them.

This family taught me that you don't have to repeat the pattern of alcoholism in the next generation. I love and appreciate all of them and still enjoy their big hugs when we see each other.

"Beloved, let us love one another, for love is from God, and whoever loves has been born of God and knows God" (1 John 4:7).

Some of you may not believe it was Jesus who was there for me. Maybe you don't know about Jesus or maybe you question if he is real. Maybe you're just checking into potentially having a relationship with Jesus. Or maybe you've had a relationship with Jesus and have strayed away or felt betrayed because of something that happened. Maybe the people in my life and the help I received are all just a coincidence. Maybe good things happen to good people, and maybe I was good enough for some good karma to come my way. Or maybe it was just dumb luck.

I don't believe in coincidences or karma or luck. Jesus loves us beyond our comprehension and asks us to love others. I believe that when we keep our hearts and minds open to Jesus, he will do good through us. I believe Jesus put amazing people in my life to do his good through them to help me. While I was mostly a recipient to start, I too made a decision to open my heart and mind and ask Jesus to work through me. And he does! I give him all the glory for good that I do. It's not something I could ever do on my own.

Although I tend to overanalyze things, there have been times in my life where I do or say something without giving it a second thought (like writing this book). Some would say it's a gut feel or intuition. I believe it's Jesus speaking clearly to me and me not doubting him. I'm going to jump forward to an example of this.

I took our daughters to church every Sunday. When they were still young, I noticed an older man was coming to church alone, and I hadn't seen him before. After several weeks, he was still coming alone. So our girls and I started sitting by him after introducing ourselves. We'd have short conversations after services. When Christmas came, our family went to the Christmas Eve candlelight service. He was there alone. As we were all walking out, I felt an urgent need to run to him and give him a hug, so I did! I caught up with him and asked him if he could use a hug. He looked at me and said, "Yes." I gave him a big hug. He started to cry, said, "Thank you, Merry Christmas!" and hurried to his car.

We continued to sit by him at church. Months later, I received a letter in the mail from him. He wrote to explain his wife had passed away, and while he wasn't ready to go back to the church they had attended together, he decided to come to our church. It was his first Christmas without her, and he was at his lowest of lows with grief when I gave him a hug that night. He tried to explain what it meant to him, but he couldn't find the words. He said he had a small gift he wanted to give us next time at church. When I unwrapped the limited edition original artwork called *Sharing Love*, he said the two little brunette angel girls reminded him of our girls and how much joy they brought to him.

Jesus is all-knowing, and he uses people who are open to do his good when someone is in need, sometimes small and sometimes big. This is what I believe, and I've been the recipient and the doer way too many times to believe anything else. It's a different kind of wonderful feeling when I do his good and understand it's not mine. I'm surprised by it, but trusting in him when I feel his prompting, I go with it. All glory to him!

"In the same way, let your light shine before others, so that they may see your good works and give glory to your Father who is in heaven" (Matthew 5:16).

9

There was a time when my mom took actions that probably saved my life. I was diagnosed with forty-nine allergies and asthma by age seven and took allergy shots for fourteen years. My dad smoked in the house and in the car, and I lived and worked on the farm with everything I was allergic to. I loved animals, even though I was allergic to all of them. The thing I'm most allergic to is horses. And oh how I wanted to ride a horse.

One evening, my mom brought my brother and I to the neighbors to visit, and they had horses. I begged and begged to ride the horse with one of their boys. My mom gave in, thinking the allergy shots would provide some protection by then because I'd been taking them for more than five years. I got up on the horse behind the boy who was going to take me, and off we went. It didn't take very long, and I could feel my throat getting itchy, and hives were popping up. I told him we better go back!

By the time I got off the horse, I was starting to have trouble breathing, so my mom quickly shuffled us into the car for the short ride home and quickly got me into the house and into the shower to wash off the dander. Then she helped me into a chair. Dad was at work. Even though I had asthma, I don't remember having any medication or inhalers for it. Every summer, I had to sleep sitting up or propped up to be able to breathe very well.

I sat in the chair, and it became harder and harder to get air into my lungs. I remember feeling panic, but the need to breathe was my focus. I was really struggling, and then I passed out. My mom told me later that she panicked but remembered that since my dad had recently developed allergic reactions to bee stings, there was an inhaler to be used for breathing emergencies. She ran for that and sprayed it into the back of my throat a few times until I came to. Clearly, I was still getting some air, even though I had passed out. My ability to breathe slowly improved. We didn't go to the hospital; we probably should have, but I feel like back then, we didn't do that as much, and there wasn't urgent care hours at the clinic.

With some quick research, I've learned that before the EpiPen came out, there was a Medihaler-Epi—both deliver epinephrine for life-threatening allergic reactions. Thank God for that because I don't know if I would have survived if that emergency inhaler hadn't been in the house. Jesus was with me. And he was with my mom, so she could think clearly about what to do, even though I cannot imagine how scared she was. I guess I can say I know what it feels like to suffocate but didn't die. God has a purpose for my life.

"'For I know the plans I have for you,' declares the Lord, 'plans to prosper you and not to harm you, plans to give you hope and a future'" (Jeremiah 29:11 NIV).

10

Our family fell into a pattern that revolved around what condition my mom was in. It's hard to explain the anxiety that comes from wondering day after day whether or not Mom would get to the point of being a mean drunk, the version of her we didn't know, and also wondering if she would be home or gone on weeknights. Sometimes I'd count the number of beer cans opening to try to anticipate when she'd turn from the mom we loved to the one we didn't know.

To nearly everyone, we probably looked like a perfect happy family. Inside our home, we were a mess. Dad was getting more angry because of what was happening, and unfortunately, he often, probably unintentionally, directed it toward my brother. Mom blamed me for everything and screamed nasty things at me. Mom and Dad argued most nights. I was Daddy's little girl, and we were both trying to help Mom. My brother was Momma's boy, and he tried to just avoid and stay out of the arguments. And my brother and I clung to each other.

To deal with stress, I ran a lot. I usually ran about three miles, down the driveway, and around the neighborhood. There was something therapeutic about it. Being outside in God's beauty, feeling the breeze, being in control of what I was doing all felt good. Sometimes I cried. Sometimes I was so angry I would scream. Sometimes I prayed. Sometimes I just tried to clear my mind and notice every little detail found in nature.

I loved swimming, too, and the Eau Galle Recreation Area was only a few miles away with a beautiful lake and beach. I'd ride my bike there and swim as often as I could, sometimes alone, and sometimes I'd find people I knew there. This is where my dad would take me and my brother fishing some mornings when we could sneak away from field work and before Dad had to leave for afternoon shift at work.

My brother and I rode the bus to school and back. When I started having confirmation class and practice for cheerleading or sports after school, we had a late bus to get home. But when I had a game or something that went later than the late bus leaving, I'd need a ride home. On those days, my mom would stop at home to pick up my brother and go to the bar. She would have me go to the bar when I was done. Then we would wait until she was ready to go home.

Being a farm girl, sometimes I thought it was kind of cool to wander around town. I remember many nights doing my homework at what used to be called Dave's Bar. Sometimes I'd want to go home so bad. If it was warm enough, I'd run the roughly four miles home, often in the dark. I guess we didn't think about or perhaps didn't even know about the risks associated with Mom being drunk and driving us home.

Jesus was there for me. He was there for all of us. He's always there for everyone and loves each and every one of us unconditionally.

"For the Lord your God is living among you. He is a mighty savior. He will take delight in you with gladness. With his love, he will calm all your fears. He will rejoice over you with joyful songs" (Zephaniah 3:17 NLT).

11

I got drunk for the first time the summer I turned fourteen. I was at a drive-in movie with my older cousin, and we were drinking Boone's Farm wine. I liked it. I don't remember ever drinking with my cousin again until I was an adult. She was and still is one of my best friends. We've had so many great times together, and she's supported me through the years. I love her *so* much!

I think it was the same summer that my parents bought a camper, and we started camping on weekends in Clam Falls. I think my dad was hoping it would be something that would help our family bond and heal, something we could do together. And, of course, we could go fishing! Oh my gosh, the time we spent there was a ton of fun! People we already knew were regular campers and how we had learned about the campground. We met many other regular campers there as well as the locals. There were quite a few kids around my age, and we quickly became good friends. We would go to the rec room to play pool and foosball. We swam in the lake, went out in the paddle boat, and had campfires. And we partied.

My parents would go to the bar across the road from the campground at night. During the day, we'd all hang out and do stuff together outside. My dad taught me how to drive the boat out on the lake, and we did a lot of fishing. I don't know if our parents knew or not that we were having our own little parties by the lake. Nobody said anything to us about it, so we kept doing it. I don't remember for sure how we got the booze. Perhaps it was snuck out of the bar by the sons of the couple that owned it.

There were no family arguments there. That would have been embarrassing with all the campers right next door. I enjoyed being away and out of the routine and struggles at home. I felt fortunate to have this group of friends there. I could just be me, and I chose not to tell them about what was going on in our family. Everybody there seemed to be having fun, so nothing about anyone in my family seemed "different" to them.

I loved tanning out on the little raft they had anchored out in the lake. Although the first fifty feet or so from shore to deeper water was full of weeds, I'd walk and swim right through it to get out to the raft and swim all over the lake. It was a sense of accomplishment and freedom to be one of the few willing to endure the weeds to get out there. And I've always loved being alone with Jesus in nature.

We camped there for two or three summers, I think. We would invite relatives or bring some of my friends from home there. We all had so much fun! God blessed us with a beautiful place with wonderful people where our family would forget about our struggles for a while.

Jesus was there for me. I was guilty of underage drinking, but Jesus kept me safe. He gave me wisdom and guided me to make good decisions to avoid other bad behaviors a young teenage girl could do. The strong foundation my parents gave me and my relationship with Jesus would keep me from completely going off the rails.

"Start children off on the way they should go, and even when they are old they will not turn from it" (Proverbs 22:6 NIV).

12

One of the biggest blessings that came as a result of growing up with an alcoholic mother is my relationship with my brother. I don't know if two siblings could be closer than we have always been. I don't remember fighting with him, unless it was when we were really young. We'd wrestle and roughhouse, but we didn't argue or fight over silly stuff like most kids.

My brother liked to sleep on the couch rather than in a room that was available upstairs. I'm not sure why because our parents' arguing had to be much louder for him in the living room than for me upstairs. So there were always pillows and blankets on our couch. We spent a lot of time on that couch. I would help him with his homework. We had to rely on each other and trust one another.

Recently, we were collectively trying to remember things that happened. We both agree some things are blocked from our memory. By the grace of God, some of the details cannot be recalled. My brother said, "I don't know how you got such good grades. We couldn't sleep at night, and I had a hard time focusing on schoolwork with everything going on." I told him I was blessed. I didn't have to try very hard to get good grades.

I asked him if he remembered Mom treating him badly directly when she was drunk. I hoped not since my dad's anger was often directed toward him. He said, "No, she said absolutely vile things to you but not to me."

My brother and I clung together, and in our own ways, we helped each other out. There was one night I came home after I had been drinking. He was upset with me and said, "I'll never drink. I would never do to my family what Mom is doing to us." And you know what? Except for part of a beer he drank when his name was called during a drinking contest at the party for my college graduation, he never drank. I think that's commendable!

Christmas was special and usually a good time for us. Our family celebrated the birth of Jesus. We'd get a tree, and I made lots of homemade Christmas ornaments for it. I still have most of them. I'd knock myself out decorating the house to make it festive. We'd help our mom bake Christmas cookies and my dad make Chex mix. Our parents bought nice gifts for us and for others. On Christmas Eve, we would always go to my godparents' (also our aunt and uncle on my mom's side) house. On Christmas Day, after church, we'd go to another uncle and aunt's house along with everyone on my mom's side, including Grandma and Grandpa.

There was only one year I remember not making it to my godparents' home for Christmas Eve. My dad had gone with Mom to the bar in town in the early afternoon. He came home drunk from drinking Tom & Jerrys. He walked in the door, saw me, and said, "Happy birthday, JoAnn!" Well, my birthday is in July, but thanks and Merry Christmas, Dad! That was the only time I remember him being drunk.

I taught my brother how to drive, and he drove my Mazda to get in his hours and take his test. We have remained close, and I thank God for him every day. There's nobody else in the world I would have chosen to go through what we did together. Jesus was there for me—for us. I pray that the millions of children with an alcoholic parent are blessed with a sibling like my brother.

"A friend loves at all times, and a brother is born for a time of adversity" (Proverbs 17:17 NIV).

"Be completely humble and gentle; be patient, bearing with one another in love" (Ephesians 4:2 NIV).

13

If the walls of my upstairs bedroom could talk, they'd tell the story of the teenage girl that lived there. That room was often my refuge. It was a beautiful room my parents had dressed up with paint, carpet, bedspread, and curtains I got to choose. Previously, it had wood floors and unpainted chipboard walls. I took great pride in decorating it and making sure it was neat and clean. I had made a bicentennial quilt that I hung on the wall. My favorite stuffed dog that my brother and I had each received as gifts years before always had a place on my bed. I had pictures of both sets of my grandparents and my Great Uncle Henry and Aunt Emma. My Raggedy Ann and Andy dolls sat on my bed, and a photo of my group at Bible Camp hung on the wall. There was some art I had made and my Bible. And my keyboard was in there. I spent hours trying to teach myself to play piano and did okay with it. Learning to play piano is still on my list of things to do.

There was the window where I waited for the aliens to come get me. There was a fuse box on the wall and one night something fiery flew from it and across my room after a lightning strike, but thankfully no fire. Another night a bat flew right across my face, close enough to touch it, and I frantically screamed for my dad who came up and killed it.

My friends and cousins would hang out there with me, and sometimes they'd sleep over. Strange, but I vividly remember standing near my dresser picking out clothes with the radio on and hearing that John Lennon was murdered.

Although most people had no clue anything was going on, I was hurting. It's hard enough for a teenage girl to have self-esteem, but when the drunk version of my mom screamed vile things about me, blamed me for everything that was wrong, and made me feel guilty about the way I looked, it was tough.

At times, I thought, *Well, I may as well go be the slut she says I am.* Being home alone a lot, I was tempted to do wrong instead of right, and I could have done anything I wanted. And I was so tired. Tired from not getting enough sleep, tired of all the arguing, afraid because the arguing was escalating to more intense levels. Emotionally, I was hurting so deeply and so badly it felt like I should be hurting physically too. That's when I started digging my nails into my skin until I bled and thinking suicidal thoughts.

I would go to really dark places in my mind. I really didn't think I could keep going and continue to deal with everything. I can honestly say at times I felt the devil working on me, tugging me to do wrong and horrible things. That scared me a lot, and I'd cry out in prayer for Jesus to protect me and be with me.

Jesus was there for me. I felt his presence, strength, and peace. I prayed and prayed and prayed while I imagined one of my hands was his holding mine. He held me tight and didn't let me go. He guided me, and although I had free will, I wanted to try to do his will more. It's in the really dark places that Jesus is with us more than ever, offering to take our pain. Every time he pulled me out of those dark places, my relationship with him grew stronger. I learned to give my problems to him and trust that he will take the load I can't bear. This didn't happen just one time. Going to dark places in my mind and Jesus pulling me out happened repeatedly, often daily.

"Peace I leave with you; my peace I give to you. Not as the world gives do I give to you. Let not your hearts be troubled, neither let them be afraid" (John 14:27).

14

When I started my freshman year in high school, I got into every activity I could. It was a great excuse for not being home, a distraction from what was happening to me and my family, and I enjoyed trying different things and spending time with other people. Unfortunately, this left my brother home alone or at the bar with my mom until I was done with what I was doing.

I was involved in softball, track, FHA, forensics, solo and ensemble, and other after-school activities. I loved cheerleading and marching band the best. I had the opportunity to make many trips to Madison with the football team, wrestlers, and marching band for state level competitions. Our marching band learned how to do the cool formations on the football field, and we took first place in the Governor's Parade. So many wonderful memories were made. We all had a really good run with a lot of winning to enjoy. I'm so thankful for all of the experiences and all the great people I experienced it with.

I don't remember my parents attending things I participated in. I think back then, a lot of parents didn't, so I don't remember feeling bad about it. I might have been the only one who went to a bar or ran home afterward, but maybe not. At some point, my cousin started living in an apartment in town, so my brother and I would sometimes go there. She was always so good about letting us hang out with her. If I remember right, she came to watch me a few times. After I turned sixteen, I could drive, and there were times I got a ride home with friends.

Back at home, it was the same repeating cycle at night. I remember thinking about how I must look to most people. I bet I looked like the happiest young lady, even with everything that was happening. Jesus was there for me. I found a way to compartmentalize my life. When I was away from the bad times at home, the peace and love from Jesus helped me to truly be happy and enjoy what I was doing. When I was in the midst of the bad times at home, the strength and refuge I found in Jesus got me through.

I was able to go to Luther Point Bible Camp a couple of times. I think our church members donated the money for at least one of the camps. Some of my friends went with me. Bible Camp was a special place where relationships with strangers were formed as we learned more about Jesus together. The campfires, singing, and time out in or near the lake were my favorites. I'm grateful for those opportunities to grow my faith and meet other people my age doing the same.

I had so many people who cared about me, and I'll never forget that. I believe God blesses us with who we need right when we need them. And Jesus is always there for us.

"And God is able to make all grace abound to you, so that having all sufficiency in all things at all times, you may abound in every good work" (2 Corinthians 9:8).

15

I was confirmed on June 3, 1979. We celebrated the public affirmation of my faith.

Our pastor held confirmation class at the parsonage (the home the church owned where the pastor lived). It was in town, so it made it easier for our parents. We could walk over there after school. We met in the garage. I feel like our pastor explained things in a way we could understand. He'd translate what the Bible says to how we could apply it as teenagers and later as adults.

My confirmation classmates and I had gone to school and Sunday school together. I enjoyed spending time with them. Our confirmation class met on Wednesdays during the school year for two years. We used *Hurlbut's Story of the Bible* for some of our studies. It was a retelling of 168 stories from the Bible. I still have it with all the underlining and notes I took in it. Our pastor would give us key messages to note, like footnotes, along with supporting Bible verses so we could look them up in our Bibles.

With these studies, I locked in my belief that the Bible is truth. The supporting Bible verses would be from different books of the Bible written by different people at different times and yet conveyed similar messages. There are even verses that are exactly the same but in different books of the Bible. The four gospels tell the story of the birth, life, death, and resurrection of Jesus. Written by different people, they're all very similar and together paint a fuller picture.

We had our share of shenanigans during class. I think our pastor allowed some of it because he wanted us to walk away with the state of mind that learning about God and reading the Bible should be something we enjoy, not something to moan about having to do.

We had a big celebration on my confirmation day with all our family and friends. My friend's mom, who had taught me to decorate cakes, made a beautiful cake for me. I received lots of gifts that I appreciated very much. The gift I was really hoping to get was a "daughter's ring" from my parents. Like a mother's ring, it would have my birthstone in the middle and my parents' birthstone on each side. I was *so* happy when I opened it. It's something so symbolic of how my parents and I are bound together in God's love, no matter what happens. As our family was unraveling, I really wanted to wear the ring as a constant reminder.

I put that ring back on my much older hand today in honor of my mom. As I'm writing this, it's Mother's Day weekend, 2022.

So many people helped me build a firm foundation in my faith in God. I have unshakable faith. Jesus was there for me. He's always been there for me and always will be. Someday I'll meet him face-to-face. By his grace and with his gift of forgiveness, I'll have eternal life with him.

> That according to the riches of his glory he
> may grant you to be strengthened with power
> through his Spirit in your inner being, so that

Christ may dwell in your hearts through faith—
that you, being rooted and grounded in love.
(Ephesians 3:16–17)

16

I already had a boyfriend when I was fourteen. He was kind and drove a very nice black Camaro. He was my friend's cousin and not from my school. He usually had two friends, who were brothers, with him when he'd pick me up to go somewhere. We'd usually meet up with more friends, including people I didn't already know, and oftentimes, my friend was with us as well. I'd stay overnight at my friend's house a lot too, so he didn't need to drive way out to my house to bring me back home.

Then, one day, when I was fifteen, we were in Martell to play some volleyball. I noticed this young man and immediately felt really attracted to him. If I remember correctly, I asked my friend who it was, and she told me his name was Nate Place. They were all family friends. I didn't talk to him that day, but I couldn't stop thinking about him.

When my boyfriend brought me home, I told him I wanted to break up. I felt awful. He had always treated me really well, but my attraction to Nate was real, and I didn't think it was fair to my boyfriend to stay with him and feel that way. I didn't win any popularity contests with my boyfriend or my friend at that time, but I did what I felt was the right thing to do.

I don't remember how much time passed until I saw Nate again. But I was at a party in Martell one night with some friends and saw him in the light of the bonfire. He was wearing a white sleeveless T-shirt or what I call a muscle shirt the way it looked on him! And I was very attracted to him. I think that was the first time we talked with one another. At some point, he called my former boyfriend to talk with him about me because they had been family friends their whole lives. I think that was very respectful.

Looking back now, we were so young! Nate was a year behind me in high school but only four months younger than me. He didn't go to my school, but we would see each other when we were with our growing group of shared friends. Later, he told me I had seen him before my first memory of seeing him at the volleyball game. I hadn't paid attention to him because I had my boyfriend, and Nate assumed I was just stuck up.

We didn't become "a couple" until later, but from the day I saw him at the volleyball game, I knew he was the one for me. Jesus was there for me. He had led me to the man I would marry and spend the rest of my life with before we even had our driver's licenses. Nate would have no idea what he was getting into with me and my family. But he loved me through it all, and oftentimes, it had to be very difficult.

"Every good gift and every perfect gift is from above, coming down from the Father of lights, with whom there is no variation or shadow due to change" (James 1:17).

17

During my sophomore year, I didn't have a boyfriend. I had already decided I only wanted Nate for my boyfriend, and he wasn't ready to have a steady girlfriend. I was reading through the autograph pages of my yearbook from that year, and apparently, some of the guys in my school were disappointed with my decision. I went on a date or two, but my heart already belonged to Nate. I'm sure some of the girls at Nate's school also hoped they could be his girlfriend.

I went to prom at my school with a friend. I'm pretty sure his mom convinced him to ask me. He was a senior, and his mom was the nurse who gave me my allergy shots every week. She was another one of my "adopted moms." I would go to their house sometimes, and she would talk with me. Her relative owned the bar where I often did my homework, and she was well aware of what was happening with my mom. She was so sweet. She had three sons and always told me she loved me and hoped I would end up married to one of her sons. She's been in heaven for quite a while now, but I hope she knew how much she helped me.

Most people probably thought I was a good girl because I was involved in so many school activities and on the "A" honor roll. I babysat for a lot of neighbors and continued to work on our farm. But there was another side of me. I partied a lot on the weekends.

My friends and I had so much fun! I still can't believe my dad would drop me (and sometimes our camper) off in Martell for the weekend. Sometimes we'd camp out "in the back forty" on our farm. We'd go to the local party spots.

A guy who graduated three years ahead of us (another friend's cousin) had his own house. If the walls of that house could talk, they'd have tons of stories to tell about all the huge parties we had there. That's where two otherwise fairly unknown bands became very popular in this area (thanks to Nate)—Rocky Burnette and the Kings. I had friends from Ellsworth, too, that I would party with. I'd see Nate at parties and enjoyed the time with him, but he wasn't sure if he wanted a girlfriend or who he would want to be his girlfriend.

A mom of one of my friends told her she didn't want her spending any more time with me. She said, "JoAnn's going to end up just like her mother."

That hurt to the core. I don't blame her. She was being a good mom and protecting her daughter. After I became a mom myself, I fully understood the love and desire to protect that a mom has for her daughters.

At home, the same repeat pattern kept going on. There just aren't words to describe the pain that came from dealing with the mean drunk version of my mom, day after day, for years. I continued to go to dark places in my mind, digging my nails into my skin and having suicidal thoughts. Sometimes I'd ride my bike to the beach to swim at dusk. Nobody was there. I'd swim halfway across the lake, kind of hoping I would get a cramp and drown with nobody there to save me.

In all of the craziness, Jesus was there for me. And I continued to pray and pray to him. While writing this, it makes me so sad to know there are millions of others who have or are going through something similar or even worse! I don't know how someone would survive it without Jesus. I pray that God's words flowing through me to write this will help someone.

"Fear not, for I am with you; be not dismayed, for I am your God; I will strengthen you, I will help you, I will uphold you with my righteous right hand" (Isaiah 41:10).

18

As my mom's alcoholism progressed, my dad and I tried so hard to convince her to stop drinking. It was affecting not only her but all of us. I prayed and prayed she would stop drinking. I begged and begged her to stop drinking. I tried to do things to help her feel good about herself, thinking if she could feel good about herself, then she wouldn't need the alcohol. She was such a lovely person when she was sober, but it was like a light switch turning on the mean drunk after enough drinks. It was like we were living with Dr. Jekyll and Mr. Hyde. Her drinking needed to stop so Mr. Hyde couldn't come out.

With the gift of manipulation that comes with alcoholism, she'd tell me she would quit drinking. I wanted to believe it so much that I did, only to be let down again and again. I'd make her things or give her a card when I thought she had quit drinking. And I'd write letters begging her to quit drinking. She kept a lot of them. Throughout my book, I'd like to share some of what I made or wrote.

I made her a "Medal of Honor for Saving Your Own Life" one time when she said she had quit drinking. I pasted a picture of Jesus with a small child praying to him. There's also sheep around him and a shepherd's hook. It made me think of the Parable of the Lost Sheep found in Luke 15. I felt like my mom was a lost sheep, and I was praying for Jesus to help her. And there's a poem on the back:

I asked God for strength that I might achieve.
I was made weak that I might learn humbly to obey.
I asked God for health that I might do greater things.
I was given infirmity that I might do better things.
I asked for riches that I might be happy.
I was given poverty that I might be wise.
I asked for power that I might have the praise of men.
I was given weakness that I might feel the need of God.
I asked for all things that I might enjoy life.
I was given life that I might enjoy all things.
I got nothing that I asked for—
but everything I had hoped for…
Almost despite myself, my unspoken prayers were answered.
I am among all men most richly blessed.

—An Unknown Confederate Soldier

The fight against alcoholism is real. My mom was the strongest person I knew, and she was losing the battle. My dad and I didn't know how to help her, and we weren't smart enough to realize arguing with her was a waste of time. Only harm would come from it, nothing good. We loved her, and we were desperate. We weren't educated about alcoholism, and although we tried to find information about it and what we could potentially do about it, it wasn't easy (there was no Internet at the time).

Jesus was there for me. He was there for all of us. He gives us free will and then weeps when we make bad choices. With the exception of my brother, we were all making some bad choices.

> Now the tax collectors and sinners were all drawing near to hear him. And the Pharisees and the scribes grumbled, saying, "This man receives sinners and eats with them."
>
> So he told them this parable: "What man of you, having a hundred sheep, if he has lost one of them, does not leave the ninety-nine in the open country, and go after the one that is lost, until he finds it? And when he has found it, he lays it on his shoulders, rejoicing. And when he comes home, he calls together his friends and his neighbors, saying to them, 'Rejoice with me, for I have found my sheep that was lost.' Just so, I tell you, there will be more joy in heaven over one sinner who repents than over ninety-nine righteous persons who need no repentance." (Luke 15:1–7, the parable of the lost sheep)

19

There were two things I remember being fairly uncommon while I was growing up. One was moms working outside the home, and another was having an inground swimming pool.

Our neighbors, the family with three kids, put in an inground swimming pool. Just when we thought our mile stretch of road couldn't be any more of an amazing place to grow up, it got even better. My brother and I were welcomed there to go swimming and spend time with the three kids. The oldest was my age and in my class. He would give me rides to and from school. We were best buddies. I helped him with his homework, and in our senior year, he became the first state wrestling champion ever in our high school.

Their middle child was a year younger than me and a year behind me in school. We were best friends and confided with each other about our family dramas. We swam in their pool a lot, and her mom would take us out to do things. She'd take us to the drive-in theater but make us get into the trunk as soon as we turned in the road to the drive-in. She'd laugh and tell us she didn't want to pay for us. And she thought it was so funny to try to scare us by taking us around the Stillwater prison and stopping the car by someone who was walking near it. Or she'd take us to a house where she'd tell a suspenseful story about the man who hung himself there. She was definitely a fun mom!

My mom was the only mom on our mile stretch of road that worked outside the home. And, oh wow, she was so jealous of the two other moms of our five neighbor kid friends who didn't work. She would leave early in the morning to go to work, knowing full well her neighbor ladies may spend the afternoon tanning in the swimming pool. My mom had worked her way from being a secretary to a computer programmer. She was smart and learned on the job. She made a very good salary. Our family lived mostly paycheck to paycheck and didn't have an abundance of money, but my parents always bought my brother and I everything we needed and helped us earn things we wanted.

I learned much later that my dad was very strict about my mom spending money on herself. So she had been going to work every day, working on the farm, taking care of us, and being told not to spend her hard-earned money on things for herself. Having been a mom who worked outside of our home myself, I can't imagine how my mom must have felt. She deserved to take time for herself and treat herself to some things. I think there are many things that led to her alcoholism, but I can definitely see how drinking may have become the one thing she did for herself.

There are so many things we don't know about other people and other families. What people see out in public and what may be happening inside a home can be very different. I think it's easy to judge others or assume someone else has it so much better than you do. I think everyone has struggles of one kind or another. And

I know there are many others who had or have it much worse than I ever have.

Jesus was there for me. He's there for you. He provides everything we need. Neighbors, friends, relatives, coworkers were all there for us when we needed them. I do my best to be there for others when they need me. This is God's desire for us that we be a community and love one another as Jesus loves us.

"A new commandment I give to you, that you love one another: just as I have loved you, you also are to love one another" (John 13:34).

20

Intervention is defined as "an occurrence in which a person with a problem (such as a alcoholism) is confronted by a group (as of friends or family members) whose purpose is to compel the person to acknowledge and deal with the problem."

My dad arranged for a professional to conduct an intervention with my mom. I remember my godparents (her sister and brother-in-law) participating along with my dad, brother, and I. The plan was to gather early in the morning and confront her before she got out of bed. I guess the thought was her mind would be more clear, and she wouldn't be feeling her best.

I don't know if alcoholics get a hangover or not. Somehow, my mom continued to get up early to go to work after being out drinking late and then arguing with my dad into the wee hours of the morning. But the professional told us that would be the best time.

He led the intervention. We were all coached to tell my mom how her drinking was affecting us and how worried we were about her. The goal was to get her to go to treatment. Her health insurance would cover the cost, and her employer would even put her on a paid leave to get the help she needed. We all poured out our hearts to her. It was really difficult to tell her about the pain we felt watching her hurting herself. It felt like she was committing a really slow suicide, one drink at a time. We told her what a wonderful woman she was without the alcohol and how we loved her so very much!

Her response was devastating. She made it very clear she knew alcohol was a problem for her and she wanted it that way. She was very angry and told us all to just leave her alone. "Get out! Get out of here!" she screamed at us. I felt the overwhelming disappointment and saw it in the faces of the others there because we loved her so much. I think we all thought if we put in the effort to bring in a professional and do exactly what they guided us to do that she would realize the best thing for her would be to seek help and get treatment to overcome the power that alcohol had over her. Now we realized she wasn't an alcoholic who wanted to stop being an alcoholic and willing to fight the battle to overcome it. She was an alcoholic who wanted to be an alcoholic and was not at all willing to try to overcome it. So now what?

I had been praying and praying for her to stop drinking and for us to figure out how to help her. This was a big lesson for me. We don't always get what we pray for. God gives us free will. We can't control other people, and God doesn't control people. I remember thinking, *Why, God? I'm praying and praying for something that's good for a good person. Why won't you answer my prayers? Why will our family continue to go through this?*

I knew my mom still had strong faith, and yet she wanted to continue being an alcoholic. She had to have known how much it hurt us. No answers, but Jesus was there for me. I still prayed to him and continued to find peace and rest only he could give me. I felt his presence and felt like I heard him say, "I'll help you through this, don't give up."

"The steadfast love of the Lord never ceases; his mercies never come to an end; they are new every morning; great is your faithfulness" (Lamentations 3:22–23).

21

God provides everything we need in so many different ways. God never says he'll provide for our wants, but he makes it clear he'll provide for our needs. And God knows what we need.

As I'm writing this, I'm feeling so much sadness and loss because our beloved almost-twelve-year-old dog, Sunny, passed away yesterday. In the past six and a half years, my husband and I have sat by the side of both of his parents, my dad, and now our dog while they suffered through their last days of illness and death. It's a painful kind of love to provide care and support for someone you love so much while helplessly watching their illness overcome them and their bodies wither away.

Jesus was there for me. Jesus was and is there for all of us. Although I feel very lonely at this moment, I am not alone. Jesus never forsakes us. Jesus is omnipresent. He experienced the pains and joys of humanity, ultimately suffering in our place as a sacrifice for our sins. The love Jesus has for us is incomprehensible and never-ending. Jesus teaches us how to love one another.

In addition to the people God gives us in our lives, he also gives us companion animals. I've been blessed to have amazing dogs all of my life. I feel like the kind of love a dog has for his or her family members is a lot like the love Jesus has for us. Even though they can't talk using words, they will comfort your pain by listening, looking at you with understanding eyes and laying their head or paw on you like a hug. They're forgiving of anything you may have done. They're loyal and will stay by your side. They will look for you when they don't know where you are. They'll protect you from harm. They'll be there when you need them most. They'll make you laugh and bring you joy. Their love is unconditional.

We shouldn't ignore or take for granted all of the ways God provides what we need and when we need it. We should accept his gifts and be grateful for them. Most importantly, we should accept the gift of eternal life. I don't believe that when we die, going into a state of nothingness is an option. I believe we will either go to heaven or go to hell. This is what the Bible says, and I believe the Bible. Many people wrote the books of the Bible over many years, and the messages to us are repeated. I believe Jesus Christ loves us unconditionally and meets us right where we are, wherever that is. I believe he yearns for a relationship with us, so much so that he died from crucifixion for the forgiveness of our sins so that if we believe in him, we will go to heaven. And I believe all dogs go to heaven.

Rejoice in the Lord always; again I will say, rejoice. Let your reasonableness be known to everyone. The Lord is at hand; do not be anxious about anything, but in everything by prayer and supplication with thanksgiving let your requests be made known to God. And the peace of God, which surpasses all understanding, will guard your hearts and your minds in Christ Jesus.

And my God will supply every need of yours according to his riches in glory in Christ Jesus. To our God and Father be glory forever and ever. Amen. (Philippians 4:4–7, 19–20)

22

When we had friends or our cousins stay overnight at our house, things were better. My parents didn't argue; or if they did, it was short. But we always knew my mom would roll in around 12:15 a.m., just before Dad would get home from work around 12:30 a.m. Mom would try to hurriedly get into bed, thinking she'd fool my dad about what time she got home.

I was talking with one of my cousins who stayed with us, and she said, "Remember how we'd watch the time and scramble upstairs before your mom got home just before your dad? We knew we needed to be out of the way before they came back."

As I mentioned before, our lives ended up revolving around what was happening with my mom. I appreciated being able to go stay at my godparents' home in Hudson for a week at a time. My cousin and I had so much fun riding our bikes around town and participating in the summer recreation program. I always appreciated a break away from the routine.

One night, the argument between my parents ended with a chair being broken into pieces. This was the point where the level of mean drunk turned to violent drunk. Thankfully, the violent drunk wasn't a daily occurrence but would come out periodically.

Since this was after our attempted intervention, I wondered if the only outcome was increased anger and no benefit. It seemed the harder we tried to help, the worse it got.

As a family, we were living a kind of new normal, I guess. There were good times and there were some really bad times. Those closest to us were becoming aware of what had been our secret, and most others still had no clue.

Jesus was there for me. I was able to wear a smile on my face and truly enjoy the good times while being fully prepared for the bad times. I started losing hope my mom would seek help to recover, and it became more of an effort to live every day with her alcoholism being a part of our lives.

It was time to run the race with endurance, trusting in the assurance of the strength and love that can only come from Jesus. I'm also forever grateful for the love and support I got from my extended family and friends.

> Therefore, since we have been justified by faith, we have peace with God through our Lord Jesus Christ. Through him we have also obtained access by faith into this grace in which we stand, and we rejoice in hope of the glory of God. Not only that, but we rejoice in our sufferings, knowing that suffering produces endurance, and endurance produces character, and character produces hope. (Romans 5:1–4)

23

Today is Monday, May 23, 2022 (at the time I'm writing this book). On both Saturday and Sunday mornings, I sat down with my laptop to write the next entry and nothing came to me. I wasn't sure where to go next with the story. I won't take full credit for writing this. All glory goes to God. I'm letting him work through me, using my life experiences, with hope that this helps someone. I'm following God's calling to do this. If I would think it through, I wouldn't do it. So I'm not thinking, I'm just doing. Jesus was there for me and will always be there for all of us. We find hope in him.

Several people have told me how they really like reading the entries as I write them. They encouraged me to keep writing and they're confident this is helping people. That's the advantage of posting one entry at a time. I've been quite overwhelmed and sometimes brought to tears with the messages and comments I've received. I look up and say, "God, you were right. I guess this is needed now."

I'm also hearing "I had no idea you were going through this." A classmate from high school said, "I really thought you were one of the few of us that actually had your shit together when we were in high school." I found "autographs" in my yearbook that confirmed I was "always so cheerful" and "always willing to listen." Sometimes, it's the people who are struggling who are there for others while hiding their own pain. And sometimes, there are really amazing people who are in pain that receive the harshest judgments unjustly.

My mom was born on this day, May 23, eighty-one years ago. And here I am, writing entry 23 of this book. I've learned I must trust God's timing. When I started paying attention, there are all kinds of occurrences in day-to-day life where God's timing is for my benefit. It may not seem like it at that moment, but later, it becomes more clear. An example was one morning when I was overwhelmed with frustration that my little girls were moving slow which would cause me to drop them off at day care late and get to work late. At the first stoplight on my commute, there was a horrible accident that had just happened. I thanked God my girls had made me late that morning or I may have been the one in the accident. There are hundreds of other examples, and with every one, I give God thanks.

I've learned and pray everyone would learn that we really don't know what people are going through. I'll never know what my mom was really going through. I highly doubt there is anybody free from pain and struggles here on this earth. Maybe if we would all back off on our judgments and extend more grace, we'd feel better, and the world would be a better place to live. This requires a lot of practice, and I haven't mastered it myself. There's only one true and final judgment for each of us. God is the judge and will decide when we die if we go to heaven or hell.

Because we're all sinners, he gave us the gift of eternal life to receive for free because Jesus paid the price for our sins on the cross.

My mom planted the seed of faith in me, nurtured my faith as a young girl, and throughout her life, I learned lessons in faith in the good times and the bad. I'm forever grateful to both of my parents for helping me to grow my faith. Jesus was there for me. Without him, I may not have been here now, and I would have missed the many blessings he's given me.

"May the God of hope fill you with all joy and peace in believing, so that by the power of the Holy Spirit you may abound in hope" (Romans 15:13).

24

My parents would host parties at our house. Sometimes family, occasionally my mom's coworkers and most often neighbors and friends, would party at our house. Growing up with this seemed fun because parties are fun. I remember my brother and I being in the midst of the "adult" parties. For many of the parties, kids were also included, so we had kids to hang out with. Being at parties with people drinking and getting drunk was normalized. Maybe this wasn't unique to us. Back then, I don't remember people worrying about being arrested for DWI as much as now.

I was looking through old photo albums, and I found several photos of my mom kissing men, not my dad, while sitting on their laps at parties in our house. And I wonder, why were these photos taken and why were they kept? When I was a teen watching it, I didn't really know what to think, but it felt really awkward. Now it's difficult to share this. But my intention is to be raw and real. And this was reality. I don't know or maybe I've blocked out the details about the inappropriate behavior of my mom while she was out and about and drunk, but I heard my parents argue about it. Alcoholism impaired her judgment, and I remember one specific incident that happened nearby where she worked.

I was witnessing the deep love my dad had for my mom slowly get replaced with resentment and anger. Both of them were in pain in different ways and for different reasons. It just kept getting worse and worse. One night, my dad locked my mom out of our house. In a drunken rage, she literally tore down the door in our kitchen. She and the door came crashing down onto our kitchen table. My fears increased as their fighting escalated. Being my mom's scapegoat became more and more painful. My dad would take out his anger on my brother more often. The level of stress and anxiety increased for all of us.

We were a mess, and yet many people still had no idea. My brother doesn't even remember us being solid as a family like I do. He was still pretty young when it all started unraveling. As a teen, I didn't exactly have a great role model for setting my moral compass. And I had free rein because my parents weren't home or because they were consumed with their problems so much that I didn't have a whole lot of boundaries set for me. My dad was pretty strict when we were growing up, so there was no doubt that there were consequences for our decisions. Dad would always tell me, "If you end up in jail, don't call me, you can sit there."

Jesus was there for me. I wasn't perfect, but I understood right from wrong given my studies of the Bible and my trusted support network of people. God provided for me, and Jesus guided me. We were still blessed with some good times as a family, but we were on this roller coaster of experiences and emotions. It was all really confusing. How could my mom be so wonderful at times and so nasty at times? She was able to bring out the best in us and the worst in us.

I kept really busy. I wore a smile on my face, got good grades, did well in all of my school activities, babysat, worked on the farm, took care of household responsibilities, went running and swimming. I had fun, went to a lot of parties, and spent as much time as I could with my friends. I went to dark places in my mind, alone in my room. And I prayed to find peace and rest I could only find from Jesus. Repeat and repeat again.

"For God gave us a spirit not of fear but of power and love and self-control" (2 Timothy 1:7).

25

When Nate asked me out the first time, he had to ask if I could pick him up because I had my license, and he didn't yet. We laugh about that to this day. Not too long after, he got his license and could pick me up. There were long distance charges to call each other, so our parents didn't want us to spend too much time on the phone. He mailed letters to me, though. I think most were written while he was doodling during class. Our relationship was still kind of on again, off again for the next couple of years—well, for him. I don't blame him. Not only were we young, but he was learning more about me and my family situation. By the end of my junior year (his sophomore year), he was ready to introduce me to his extended family at his brother's graduation party. And for the next year and a half, we were "a couple" most of the time.

I liked spending time with his family. And we'd have parties at their house when his parents would go away for the weekend. I met a lot of new fun people. He spent a lot of time in Spring Valley because his Martell friends went to my school (well, and I was there). Our group of shared friends grew, and we all had a lot of fun together.

Although Nate saw me as others saw me, he also came to know me as I was at home. I don't know how many times I called him, sobbing and begging him to come and get me out of my house. Almost always, he'd come over, no matter how late. Sometimes we'd just sit out in his car in the driveway and sometimes he'd take me for a drive. He'd hold me and tried to console me. If he couldn't come over, he'd stay on the phone with me until he was comfortable and I had settled down. He'd reassure me and try to build me back up as I was feeling crushed.

He'd come over, and sometimes my mom would stay home to play cards with us, usually with some small bets placed. It was nice to have another person that made being home a little better. At times, though, he witnessed the bad things. It's really quite amazing to me that he stuck it out with me. His life wasn't perfect either, and immersing himself in my mess took a lot of courage. And it's completely understandable why it took him longer than me to decide we should be together.

I have to admit that, ultimately, I picked a fight with the other girl he was interested in during our "off" times. One of his family friends had become one of my best friends (she still is, and I'm so grateful for her; we've made countless wonderful memories together through the years). I was at her house, and we were planning to go to Nate's birthday party together. This was at a time our relationship was "off." My friend was going to back me up on my plans to confront this girl. Mission accomplished. I fought for my man, and nobody got hurt. Oh my gosh, so funny. But since then, we've been together. God bless Nate.

Jesus was there for me. There was no doubt in my mind I had found the man I wanted to spend my life with at a very early age. And I believe Jesus was with Nate too. Seriously, how many young men would be willing to choose a relationship with someone like me with all my struggles? I found an old picture from when he picked me up to go to both of our proms. He was a junior, and I was a senior. It reminded me so much of the countless times he'd come to get me out of my house. Unlike all of those times, for prom, we were both happy and had a lot of fun!

"Love bears all things, believes all things, hopes all things, endures all things" (1 Corinthians 13:7).

26

Throughout the Bible, there are many stories about miracles. The man-made definition of a miracle is an event that appears inexplicable by the laws of nature and so is held to be supernatural in origin or an act of God. I believe miracles are an act of God; some are noticed and some are not.

During my junior year, I remember driving around a lot with my friends. Some nights, we'd drive around all night and never go to a destination. We may end up parked in a field or at the end of a road, but generally, we'd just drive around. Sometimes we'd have booze with us and sometimes not. For several of my friends, phone calls had long distance charges, and we didn't have Internet or cell phones. So we looked for something to do together. Maybe we were exerting our new independence with our driver's licenses.

One of my friends had a Chevette. It had a stick shift. She wasn't really a fan of driving a stick shift, so when we'd drive around in her car, she'd sometimes let me drive. My dad had me learn to drive using a stick shift. We'd load that little Chevette up with the few girls that fit and drive around for hours, listening to REO Speedwagon. My friend always had a curfew.

The weekend of Easter, 1981, I was invited to drive around with my friends in the Chevette on Saturday night. I really wanted to go, but I decided I should be good and stay home so I could go to Easter church service in the morning. I got up Easter morning and went to church. Soon after, I got a phone call. My friends I was invited to go with had been in a horrible car accident.

My friend who was the passenger got a broken collarbone and bruises. She was able to walk to the nearest house and cry out my other friend's name before she passed out. Thank God. So the EMTs knew to look for another person. My other friend who was driving was in bad shape. She was in a coma for six days with a traumatic brain injury, broken pelvis, and other injuries. She had been in a hurry because she was running late to make it home by curfew. She lost control after hitting some frost heaves in the road.

Jesus was there for them. My friend, who was the passenger, was spared from cuts by her leather jacket, which was full of glass splinters. My friend who suffered the severe injuries endured a long recovery, having to learn things like walking again. She has a very strong faith, and we remain friends. I chatted with her recently to make sure I shared correct details about this miracle. It wasn't until nine years after the accident that she could remember some details. My friends now have children and grandchildren of their own.

Jesus was there for me. I didn't go and, therefore, wasn't in the accident. I often wonder, what if I had gone with them? Would I have been driving, and if so, would the accident have happened? If I was with them, how badly would I have been injured? I trust that Jesus guided me to my decision to stay home so I could go to church. I wish I had been there more for my friend as she was recovering, but she graciously assured me that it's okay. There's no doubt in my mind that Jesus protected and healed my friends.

Accidents and other bad things happen on this earth. I believe God doesn't make bad things happen. I don't know why some people are spared and some are not. Perhaps the answer is much larger than our minds can comprehend. I believe God provides everything we need when bad things happen and even brings good out of bad.

"But if I were you, I would appeal to God; I would lay my cause before him. He performs wonders that cannot be fathomed, miracles that cannot be counted" (Job 5:8–9 NIV).

27

In Spring Valley, where I grew up, there's an annual celebration called Dam Days. This was to celebrate the completion of the Eau Galle Dam and Reservoir with its dam, lake, recreation areas, and channel improvements. It was authorized by the Flood Control Act of 1958 as a result of repeated flooding in the Spring Valley area. The 649-acre project was built from 1965–1968.

In September 1981, it was decided that Dam Days royalty would be selected for the first time in over ten years. So I decided to enter as a candidate. I was trying to stay as busy as possible, and this was another thing I could do. The selection process was fun and friendly with the candidates supporting one another. I really wasn't thinking I would be selected.

The second runner-up was announced, and then first runner-up. The princesses had been selected. Then they announced the queen. It was me, and I remember thinking, *Wait, what?* I felt so honored as a crown was placed on my head. A beautiful new float had been built for us to ride on in parades for the next year. I wish I could remember who hauled us and the float around. It was a kind and generous man who volunteered to do it.

Riding on the float in that first Dam Days parade, newly crowned, down the streets of the town that I had wandered aimlessly around on a lot felt really good. My family, including my godparents and other extended family members, came to watch. I was in the local newspaper and also in the town where my grandpa (Mom's dad) lived, listed as his granddaughter. He was in his nineties, and I know it made him very proud. He was well aware of my mom's alcoholism.

Then I received a letter in the mail from our high school principal. I still have it and would like to share some excerpts:

> Congratulations on being selected Miss Spring Valley. Being the first queen in over ten years is quite an honor. It is also quite a responsibility as you will now be representing your family, your school and the entire community. Many hours will be spent representing our area.
>
> Your activities over the next year will set the standard for all of your successors.
>
> Congratulations and good luck. I am sure a finer person could not have been found to be named Miss Spring Valley.

I remember feeling a little bit sick to my stomach when I read that. Representing my family—yikes, I'm the daughter of an alcoholic that more and more people know about. Representing my school and the entire community—uh-oh, although I hid my mischievous side pretty well, that felt like a lot of pressure. Struggling with self-esteem, I certainly thought the other candidates were better than me.

Being Miss Spring Valley for a year was an amazing experience, especially because one of the princesses happened to be my best friend. We were like sisters, and some people thought we were! We were classmates, cheerleaders, and in band together. I love her to this day. I noticed in my yearbook, she was the only one who wrote "May God bless you and keep you safe and happy."

I was seventeen and already realized it's a choice to make. I could choose to be a victim, carry baggage around, feel sorry for myself, and blame making bad choices on a "hard life." Instead, I chose to take full responsibility for my life—the good and the bad. Imperfect for sure, but I believed (and still do) that every day I have a choice about how I'm going to feel and what I'm going to do, no matter what gets thrown at me. Jesus was there for me. He's there for you. He's there for everyone, especially when we're faced with personal challenges. He yearns for us to be near to him, trust him, and give to him what we can't handle. Let Jesus bless you.

"Arise, for it is your task, and we are with you; be strong and do it" (Ezra 10:4).

28

I had the best senior year a girl could ever have. I was a cheerleader for football and wrestling. The football team went to state playoffs, and two of my good friends went to state in wrestling. My friend (and neighbor) won the state wrestling championship, first one ever in our school. I was in band, marching band, and on the band board. Our band went on a trip to the Wisconsin Dells, and I went to state solo and ensemble. I was in Aeolian choir, the letterpersons club, FHA, ranked in the top four of my class while taking advanced classes, and was Miss Spring Valley.

I was having fun at parties without getting caught and solidifying a relationship with the man I knew I wanted to spend the rest of my life with, still working on the farm, babysitting, and saving money so I could buy a car. Life at home just kept getting worse, though. While I was busy trying to live life to the fullest, my mom's life was falling apart.

This is some of her own description (that I found later) of losing her life to alcohol.

> I was hiding booze in closets, cupboards, clothes hampers, and dresser drawers. I lied to my husband about where our money went. I'd

write a check to the store for extra cash back. I denied that I drank as many drinks as my husband said. I'd say I had a few drinks. He was right when he said I had more than a few. When I had been drinking I did the easy jobs at work so as not to blow a big one and called in sick when I felt hungover. My main priority was to get to the bar and make sure I had enough booze on hand to get through the night. I wasn't punctual for the kids' school events (remember my brother still needed rides) and I would avoid going to them. I risked the lives of my kids taking them home after school events. I couldn't remember who I was talking to and found out later what a fool I made of myself. I quit going to church because I got drunk the night before.

My mom and dad continued to fight every night She lost touch with her real friends as she spent her time with her so-called bar "friends." My dad and I continued to try to get her to stop drinking. She did not want to quit. She admitted she was an alcoholic and said she liked it that way. One time, my godmother and aunt (her sisters who didn't live in our town) walked right into the bar to confront her. They brought her out of the bar and to my cousin's apartment which was nearby. They begged and pleaded with her to stop drinking. They pointed out she was starting to lose everything—her husband, kids, job, and herself. They loved her so much and knew full well what a wonderful and beautiful woman she was. Their hearts were breaking. My mom told them the same thing she told us.

Her mom had passed away, but her dad was still doing pretty well in his nineties. He worried about her. My mom was the youngest of seven and really close to her dad. She was definitely still Daddy's little girl. We all felt incredibly helpless as nothing we said or did seemed to help her. We prayed and prayed.

Jesus was there for me. Our prayers weren't being answered the way we wanted or when we wanted. God gives us all free will. I think Jesus probably felt helpless too and cried like we cried. Even though he couldn't force her to want to overcome her alcoholism, he was there for her and there for everyone who cared about her.

"Let no one say when he is tempted, 'I am being tempted by God', for God cannot be tempted with evil, and he himself tempts no one. But each person is tempted when he is lured and enticed by his own desire" (James 1:13–14).

29

Emotional pain is challenging and can be easily ignored by others because it's "invisible." It's repetitive and compounds over time. It's anticipated and yet unpredictable. It can be addictive, and yet we feel like we should be able to just shake it off. It can feel unbearable at times.

Alcoholism is known as a "family illness," and I agree. My mom's alcoholism was clearly hurting her, but it was also causing issues that would last a lifetime and need to be addressed by each one of us.

We were six years into my mom's alcoholism having control over her life and bouncing from the wonderful version of her to the mean drunk version of her. It was becoming more clear she had no interest in trying to recover and stay sober. Dealing with the pain of feeling like we're losing her and being the recipient of her drunken meanness, all while loving her so much, led to feelings of desperation.

This is difficult to write, and I pray my dad will forgive me for sharing this, but it was one of the worst nights of my life. It started like a thousand other nights. My parents were arguing after my dad got home from work. I was lying in bed, awakened for the duration of the argument in the middle of the night and praying to Jesus to try to manage my anxiety.

This argument seemed to last a really long time and kept escalating, getting louder with nastier accusations. Then I heard a zipping sound at the bottom of the stairs that led to my bedroom. I knew what was kept there in the corner where the stairs took a turn—our guns. I heard my dad say, "I can't take this shit anymore! I don't want to live if this is what our life is going to be." As he was taking the gun out of the case, he was crying. As I heard him loading a shotgun shell into the gun, I wanted to jump out of bed, run down there, and stop him!

I couldn't move! Why couldn't I move? I needed my dad! He was the one who supported me. How was I going to stop him from killing himself if I couldn't move? It felt like forever, anticipating the gun going off while lying frozen in my bed. I don't even know if I was breathing. We were already losing Mom, and now Dad too? What were we going to do? Then finally I heard him eject the shell. He was sobbing and said, "Damn it, my kids need me."

Thank you, Jesus! Yes, yes, we do need you, Dad. Although I could move again and I wanted to run down and hug him, I stayed in my bed. I really didn't know what to do. I understood the dark place my dad had gone. I was exhausted with adrenaline pumping through my body. I don't think I slept the rest of the night. In the morning, I got up and went to school, wearing a smile on my face the best I could. What had happened was never talked about in our family again until I talked with my brother after I started writing this book. My brother and I trust God, and my brother has entrusted me to write what I feel I need to write.

Being paralyzed with fear is a real thing. I've never been paralyzed with fear again nor before that night. Jesus was there for me.

Jesus was there for my dad and for all of us. I was blessed and so grateful to have had my dad in my life for another forty years. I was Daddy's little girl until the day I laid my head on his chest, held his hand, and cried while he took his last breath. I don't know what I would have done without him in my life.

"The Lord your God is in your midst, a mighty one who will save; he will rejoice over you with gladness; he will quiet you by his love; he will exult over you with loud singing" (Zephaniah 3:17).

30

High school graduation day came on May 16, 1982. I graduated with honors, ranked fourth in my class. We were a small class of seventy-five people but one of the larger classes to graduate from the school. I loved being able to know everyone in my class. As one of the cheerleaders, the football players felt like family, the same for the wrestlers. After four years, we had spent many hours on buses together. Most everyone in our class got along really well.

Our class motto was "Only as high as I reach can I grow, only as far as I seek can I go, only as deep as I look can I see, only as much as I dream can I be" (Karen Ravin).

We had a big party at our farm with all my relatives, neighbors, and friends. It was a lot of fun, and everything went smoothly. One thing for sure, we were good at hosting parties. If I remember correctly, everyone had their graduation party with family on the day of graduation, and then a lot of my classmates gathered for a party later that night.

I was all set to start college in the fall at Lakewood Community College (now called Century College) for data processing (now probably called computer science or programming). Since my mom had worked her way into being a programmer, I thought being a programmer would be good for me too. I knew I didn't want to be a farmer, and my dad told me I wouldn't want to work in a factory like him.

Believe it or not, I didn't move away from home as quick as I could. Jesus was there for me. I always pray for guidance. I welcomed Jesus into my heart and mind to guide me, and he put people I needed in my life too. There's an unexplainable peace that comes with trusting God. I'm so grateful I learned that at a young age. I was confident God would provide everything I needed to get out there and build a beautiful life with Nate while still feeling responsible to help my family at home.

My plan was to continue living at home through two years of college and get an associate's degree. I would drive my mom's car and drop her off at work on my way to college and pick her up on the way home each day. I had received a scholarship that would cover the cost of one semester, and my parents would pay for the rest. I thought that was really generous and nice of them.

I wanted to be there for my brother who was just starting high school. I was afraid to leave him there without me, not knowing what might happen in our dysfunctional home. I have to admit, though, a big reason I continued to live at home was I wanted to be close to Nate. He had his senior year in high school to complete yet. There were still plenty of good parties to go to on the weekends, and both Nate and I would be eighteen soon and old enough to go to the bars. And I was able to continue babysitting and saving money to buy a car.

I'm happy I saved the things from graduation that were special to me. I saved the card from my parents. That's the last card I have that was signed from both of them. And the picture taken on that day is the last picture I have with both of them.

> I will praise the LORD, who counsels me; even at night my heart instructs me. I keep my eyes always on the LORD. With him at my right hand, I will not be shaken. Therefore my heart is glad and my tongue rejoices; my body also will rest secure, because you will not abandon me to the realm of the dead, nor will you let your faithful one see decay. You make known to me the path of life; you will fill me with joy in your presence, with eternal pleasures at your right hand. (Psalm 16:7–11 NIV)

31

My mom's alcoholism continued to consume more and more of her life. She became more difficult to try to maintain a relationship with but also had some good times when the mom we used to know would shine. She continued to make it clear that she knew she was an alcoholic and liked it that way. Nothing we could say or do would change her mind at all.

My dad decided he had one more thing to try. He informed our local law enforcement that she was driving home from the bar drunk nightly, usually at the same time. He told them he was concerned that she was putting herself and others at risk. My dad had researched the penalties for DWI and found out an alcohol assessment with possible court order for outpatient treatment could be included in the sentence. He knew she could still get to work because I was driving her to her workplace on my way to and from college.

Then one night, she was arrested for DWI and put in jail. When she made her one call to my dad, asking him to go bail her out, he told her she could stay there. By this time, my dad and I were learning about the concept of "tough love." We had learned alcoholics have "a bottom" that they need to hit before they'll seek help. Of course, we didn't know where my mom's bottom was going to be.

The next morning, he called in to her work to let them know she wasn't going to be in that day. Later, he picked her up, and nothing really changed. I prayed and prayed for her sentence to include treatment.

Her court date came, and she was sentenced with a fine and an alcohol assessment. Her assessment resulted in court-ordered outpatient treatment. Yes! I had convinced myself if she would just get treatment, she would understand she needed to stop drinking. What I hadn't thought of was I'd be the one who needed to drive her to outpatient treatment two or three nights a week for a few months (I can't remember how many). Outpatient treatment was at night, and my dad worked nights. So on those days, I was driving an hour each way to her work and my college and then forty minutes each way to take her to treatment at night.

I don't think she ever stopped drinking during treatment. She cut back to make it look good, but I'm almost certain she was drinking from her hidden stash, and maybe someone was helping her keep her hidden stash full. Needless to say, treatment did nothing to help her stop drinking because she did not want to stop drinking.

I had my hopes so high and had worked so hard to encourage her. So when it didn't work, I was devastated. My dad too. At this point, we realized we were pretty much out of options to try. Everyone had been trying, and nothing was working. Jesus was there for me. Although my prayers went unanswered the way I wanted them to be answered, I knew I had to keep my faith and keep praying. I didn't know what else to do. I felt completely helpless, wondering when and how this would end.

"Those who obey him will not be punished. Those who are wise will find a time and a way to do what is right, for there is a time and a way for everything, even when a person is in trouble" (Ecclesiastes 8:5–6 NLT).

32

In college, one of my technical writing assignments was to write a paper for a target audience with a specific purpose. We were to plan, research, and then write the paper with footnotes, citing our sources. I saved this paper and have reread it many times. I feel like it's pretty solid advice from someone still a teenager. Jesus was there for me. He provided so many means for me to learn to cope with my mom's alcoholism.

This paper will be the content of three entries in my book. It's titled "Learning to Live with an Alcoholic Parent," and the target audience is children between the ages of twelve and seventeen who have an alcoholic parent. Page 1:

> I am the child of an alcoholic parent. I know
> it is very hard to admit your parent is an alcoholic,
> but the hardest thing to do is to learn to live with
> your alcoholic parent. You are forced to cope with
> problems that other people your age don't have.
> Most books or pamphlets I have looked at or read
> give information about the problems that children
> of alcoholics face. That's information you and I
> already know. What we really need is help finding

answers and solutions to our problems. I would like to share with you some answers and solutions I have found by talking with other people who are either related to an alcoholic or are "dried out" alcoholics, by doing a lot of reading, and especially by learning from experience.

Before you can learn to live with an alcoholic, you must first understand what alcoholism is. Alcoholism is a health problem—a physical and emotional sickness of the alcoholic. Nobody is certain of its cause. Alcoholism is also defined as a "family disease" because of the ill effects it has on the family of the alcoholic.

There is no need to feel alone. Recent statistics indicate that there are approximately ninety-five million adult drinkers in the country, and perhaps nine million of them drink to excess. More than thirty-six million Americans are victims of the effects of the disease. You are one of the thirty-six million people who are affected by alcoholism. Anyone can become an alcoholic, but it is most common in the thirty-five to fifty-five age group. The majority of alcoholics are within the age range of parents who have children living at home.

If you feel like it is your fault that your parent is drinking a lot, don't. You may never know the real reason for your parents' drinking. Sometimes there isn't a reason. Your parent may blame you and accuse you of many different things that aren't true. Don't ever let yourself believe any of it. Your parent knows what he or she is doing is wrong and many times will do anything to make himself or herself feel better, even if it means hurting you, by telling you it's your fault that he or she drinks.

If you have many mixed emotions such as love and hate, fear and pity for your parent, it doesn't usually do much good to try to sort them. Your mixed emotions are caused by your parents' mixed behaviors. Sometimes your parent may act very affectionate, loving, and caring—usually when he or she is fairly sober. This is the time when you feel love for him or her. Other times, your parent may neglect you, blame you, or be mean to you—usually when he or she is drunk. This is the time when you feel hate for him or her.

Mixed in with these emotions, you probably fear your parent may hurt himself/herself or someone else or they may someday kill himself/herself. You may feel helpless because you don't know what to do about the situation. All of these emotions mixed together are okay. You can't help the way you feel, but a lot of the time, it helps to talk to somebody about your feelings. Don't keep everything to yourself, and remember there is nothing wrong with your mind. You're feeling all of these different emotions because of the way your parent is acting.

33

Page 2 of my paper titled "Learning to Live with an Alcoholic Parent":

Don't be ashamed of your parent. You don't have to try to hide it or make any excuses for your parent. Doing this will hurt you more than help your parent. The best thing to do is admit that your parent is an alcoholic. I'm not saying you should advertise it, but by letting people who are close to you know, you can better learn to cope with the problem with their help. These people most likely already know your parent is an alcoholic, so when you ask to talk to them about it, they won't be shocked. Once you admit it, you'll be surprised at the number of people who either are or know an alcoholic.

Having an alcoholic parent may force a great amount of responsibility on you. You may have to do extra household chores or take care of your younger brothers or sisters. You may feel angry because nobody else your age has these responsibilities, but just think of yourself as being more mature. Having a great deal of responsibility may not be right, but there may not be anything you can do about it. Don't be bitter because of your responsibilities because it may ruin your outlook on all responsibilities for the rest of your life. Try to keep a good outlook on life!

Having these responsibilities may make you feel very independent. This is okay to a certain point, but don't let yourself think you don't need anybody. You do! If you let yourself become very independent, it may cause some big problems later in your life when you start getting into a male-female relationship. It is very hard to love somebody who acts like he or she doesn't need you. Also, being very independent may make you feel like you can't trust anybody but yourself, and trust is a very important part of a relationship. Don't let what is happening now ruin your life.

Another problem you may be facing is seeing your parents fight. Maybe they fought before your parent started drinking, and maybe not. If it seems like they're fighting a lot now, I can almost guarantee it is because of alcoholism. An alcoholic, especially when drunk, becomes very unpredictable and very hard to get along with. Remember your other parent is under a lot of stress also. He or she is being hurt by the alcoholic also. Try to understand why he or she is upset, but at the same time, try to stay out of all fights between your parents if possible. Both parents may be encouraging you to take their sides. You should not be forced to choose one parent over the other. Choosing a side can be a very painful experience, and you can save yourself from pain by going in your room and closing the door or maybe going outside for a walk if it's safe. Another possibility is to call somebody and go to stay at their house for a night. Whatever you do, don't get the idea of physically hurting yourself because you're angry. Please don't do that. It won't help anything.

Remember, you have your own life to live—eventually apart from your alcoholic parent. You won't have to deal with this problem all your life. Also, don't get the impression that all married couples fight like your parents do. Your parents loved each other and maybe still do. The fighting between your parents is largely a result of being angry at the illness. Alcoholism can change people very much.

34

Page 3 of my paper titled "Learning to Live with an Alcoholic Parent":

One-half of the children of alcoholics later become victims of the illness themselves. Many experts have tried to figure out why, and no one has found the actual reason. One of the more popular theories is the biosocial theory. It includes reasons such as personality, inheritance, and culture. People who agree with this theory believe a person may inherit a state of mind that makes that person more likely to get the illness.

When exposed to the right environment, especially the frustration of having to cope with an alcoholic parent, chances of getting the illness are greater. Don't get the idea that drinking alcohol is bad for everybody. When you are legal age, it is okay to drink socially if you like. By this, I mean having a drink or two when you go out. Alcohol is only damaging when is it abused. But always watch yourself because you are a prime candidate for becoming an alcoholic. Don't ever do that to yourself! Keep limits on your drinking or don't drink at all. Remember that no matter what anybody tells you, you don't have to drink if you don't want to.

Don't allow your schoolwork to slip. By doing this, you are only hurting yourself. You cannot make up for those losses, and you'll probably continue to be a poor student. If school gets boring or you can't keep your mind on it, get involved with some school activities. They make school much more fun and will also help you keep your mind off your problems at home.

If you want to talk about your feelings and problems with someone who shares them and will really understand, join Alateen. Alateen is a group of children who have alcoholic parents who get together to talk about it. Alateens do not criticize the alcoholics' behavior but learn to live less affected by it. They learn they are not crazy, in spite of having been told that by their alcoholic parent. These meetings could really help you learn to live with your alcoholic parent.

Instead of directing your anger and frustration at your parents and other authority figures—which may get you into trouble—release any built up anger and frustration by exercising or writing everything you would like to say to somebody on paper. This may sound dumb, but it really helps release your anger. Don't keep anger and frustration inside or let it build up. This could result in a really bad tantrum or a continual anger at everybody.

I hope you'll be able to use some of my suggestions on how to learn to live with your alcoholic parent. Think about yourself and keep your goals and ambitions in focus. Everything that's happening now doesn't have to affect your own future if you don't let it. Sometimes it's hard not to quit trying, but you've got to stay strong for your own sake. One of the most important things you can do for yourself is to never, ever start drinking heavily. You've seen what alcoholism has done to your parent, and I'm sure you don't want it to happen to you!

That's the end of my paper, other than some references to resources for help that I included. One of the things that's missing from my paper is Jesus. I wonder why I didn't include him or any reference to my faith. Was it because I wasn't yet comfortable in sharing my faith? Was it because it was a college paper, so I didn't think it was appropriate? I don't know and don't remember. Jesus was there for me. That alone is the reason I'm here today and living a life filled with abundant blessings. He provided me with everything I needed. I had to take the initiative to recognize and leverage what I was given. I practiced accepting the things I could not change and changing the things I could. Jesus gave me wisdom and resources to learn the difference.

"If any of you lacks wisdom, let him ask God, who gives generously to all without reproach, and it will be given him" (James 1:5).

35

This is my story. I thank God it's not the worst story. Unfortunately, there are millions of people with stories way worse than mine. There's so much evil in the world and so many forms of addiction and abuse. Worst of all, children suffer. I would guess that everyone has a story. Pain is inevitable in this world. If you're a child of an alcoholic, you may feel like our stories have some similarities. It seems like the journey is similar for most alcoholics. Some overcome it and some do not.

It's still unclear to me why I felt such a strong calling from God to write my story. God will work in us and through us. There's power in personal testimony, and I believe that having a relationship with Jesus is the most important thing in everyone's life. Jesus is our salvation. I can't imagine how alone and hopeless I would feel without Jesus. I pray that if you don't have a relationship with Jesus that you'll consider it.

I once read that our greatest purpose in life often comes from our greatest pain. It's never been quite clear what that means for me. Perhaps writing about how Jesus was there for me through my life experience is a part of my purpose and a way for God to work through me to help others.

What if instead of keeping our pain to ourselves, we all found ways to use it to help others? A lot of people do, but what if everyone did in some small or big way? Jesus said we should love one another, and through love, we can help one another. The impacts of loving someone who is an alcoholic is something I know and understand. But I would not fully understand the impacts of other forms of addiction and abuse. Only someone who has gone through it would.

There's risk in trying to help others. Sometimes it works out and sometimes it doesn't. A lot of time and energy can be spent trying to help someone. It only helps if the person you're trying to help wants the help. It usually means the person will need to make changes, and maybe they're not willing to make the changes. This makes me wonder how Jesus may feel. He knows what we need and he's always near, wanting to help. But if we don't want him or his help, then we can reject it. It's really tough when someone you love is hurting himself/herself, doesn't want to make changes, rejects or avoids your help, and you're left helplessly watching them continue to hurt himself/herself.

Love is a powerful emotion. Alcoholism is a powerful illness. As a parent and grandparent now, I would do anything to protect my kids and grandkids because I love them so much. Having never been an alcoholic myself, I can only imagine how the power of alcoholism can be more powerful than love itself. It's hard to wrap my mind around the fact that my mom would "choose" getting drunk, which made her say and do hurtful things to the family members she loved. We loved her despite her illness, but it wasn't enough for her to want to make changes to try to overcome her alcoholism.

I could see over time as my dad's love for my mom was being replaced with frustration and anger that he was starting to give up. I was determined to continue to try to help her. I didn't have any great ideas or answers. I kept hoping and praying that if my brother and I continued to show her how much we loved her and didn't want her to die from her alcoholism that maybe the power of her motherly love for us could overpower her alcoholism. Perhaps this is the point at which I became an enabler more than anything else. Jesus was there for me. I found strength to keep fighting this battle with my mom's alcoholism, even while she didn't have any desire to try.

"And let us not grow weary of doing good, for in due season we will reap, if we do not give up" (Galatians 6:9).

36

I cannot even imagine the internal struggles an alcoholic must go through. I can attest to the power of a mother's love and the never-ending and unrestrained instinct to protect and nurture her children. When the power of alcoholism creeps in, there must be a raging battle within. I found proof of my mom's internal battle. When I was young and before alcohol started taking over Mom's life, I had an assignment to write a paper titled "The Person I Admire Most." I wrote it about my mom. I found it folded and in her one and only photo album. It clearly was crumpled up and straightened back out multiple times. I pictured my mom dealing with her internal battle reading my paper and then crumpling it up with her angry hands. And then straightening it back out, only to do it again later.

For more than forty years, I've periodically checked in on the most recent research available regarding alcoholism. How do we know someone is an alcoholic? The criteria provided by research have varied, but the one that has always made the most sense to me has remained consistent: consuming alcohol interferes with work, school, family, or other responsibilities. The addition of another criterion provides more clarity: continuing to drink alcohol despite negative impacts on relationships or career. For me, personally, this is when I stop.

There have been many times in my life where I think I can have one or two drinks when we go out, which is fine for a while. But, inevitably, I moved into the early stage of alcoholism, which is binge drinking. I don't drink often, but when I do, I drink too much. Then, inevitably, I say or do something that negatively affects someone in my family—"consuming alcohol interferes with family." Then I stop, sometimes for seven or eight years. But then I think I'm good to have one or two drinks when we go out, and I repeat the cycle I just described. It's been almost two years since I stopped again. This time, I'm determined to never start again.

Another criterion that makes sense to me is "needing to drink more alcohol over time to achieve the same level of intoxication." I do this. That's when one or two drinks becomes more over time, and then I'm a binge drinker again. If a feeling of intoxication is the goal, then the risk of becoming a chronic alcoholic increases. The feeling of intoxication can be very appealing, whether it's to numb feelings, deal with stress, calm down, have fun, forget about everything, escape reality, or so many other things. It's a temptation for sure. I need to accept that I'm at risk of becoming an alcoholic, and I will not let that happen to me. I'm tired of finding myself in a cycle. It's something I can control and will.

Jesus was there for me. I've made it this far without alcoholism taking over my life. I do meet the criteria for being an early stage alcoholic who doesn't drink alcohol right now. I regret not making the decision to stop the cycle a long time ago. Being in a cycle of flirting with the risk of becoming an alcoholic for the last forty-plus years created stress that could have been avoided. But we live and we learn. We all have our own journeys through life.

I continue to pray for guidance. I believe that without the peace, hope, and love that can only be found in Jesus that I would not be who I am today. The love that Jesus has for us never fails. God loves us so much that he sent his only son, Jesus, to live a perfect life as an example and then die a grueling death on a wooden cross for all our sins. I believe the love a parent has for their children never fails. I know my mom always loved me (us). Alcoholism robbed her and us of the beautiful relationship we once had and could have had. I have a tattoo of my life verse, three simple words but oh so powerful!

"Love never fails" (1 Corinthians 13:8 NIV).

37

While commuting with my mom, leaving early in the morning, the whole car smelled of booze. She usually slept on the way to work, and I wondered how in the world she could get her work done. By the time I picked her up, all she could think about was making sure she could get to the bar in time for happy hour. At least I could get most, if not all, of my homework done while I was at college because the drives home felt really stressful.

I was taking care of household responsibilities, helping my brother as needed and spending time with Nate. My parents continued to argue at night. And if I remember correctly, by this time, we were doing very little as a family. We weren't doing much with our relatives or our parents' friends like we used to. My mom and dad had stopped going out dancing. My dad busied himself with work at his job and at home on the farm. He was always working and sure expected the rest of us to be working too.

It was Nate's senior year in high school. I'd go watch him play football, which I usually couldn't do while I was still cheerleading. He'd already been working since before he got his license so he could have a car. I think it felt a bit awkward for Nate still being in high school while I was in college, especially the night we were "parking" in a remote area way off of the main road and a Pierce County officer pulled in with his lights on. The officer questioned Nate and I sep-arately. He asked me if Nate was forcing me to do anything I didn't want him to do, and I said no. He asked me my name, and when I told him, he said, "Oh, I know your dad." I thought I'd hear about it later but never did. After he left, we had to chuckle a little bit because I was the adult, already eighteen, and Nate wasn't yet at that time.

Just three months into his senior year, Nate turned eighteen. The legal age to drink alcohol was eighteen then, so in addition to the parties, we could go to the bars and listen to bands. There were so many awesome bands playing back then, and we sure had a lot of fun.

I didn't have my own car yet, so Nate was always coming to get me. Although much less often, I would still call him sobbing and ask him to come to get me out of the house when I felt like I couldn't be there any longer. As my dad was starting to give up on trying to help my mom, there was less arguing, and the arguments grew less intense. I'm sure he would have wanted nothing more than for her to overcome her alcoholism and rebuild their relationship, but it was becoming more clear that probably wasn't going to happen.

While I really wanted to help my mom, I was at a loss for how to do it. At that time, there was no legal way to force someone into treatment. I really believed that if she would go to an inpatient treat-ment program that her mind would be cleared enough to realize she was losing everything important in her life, and she would want to get her life back from the grip of alcohol. But nothing we could say or do would motivate her to do that.

Jesus was there for me. I continued to practice accepting what I could not change and changing the things I could. I was focusing more energy on plans for my future with Nate. I worked really hard in college and found comfort knowing in the near future I would be moving away from home. I found a photo of Nate and I from when he had his senior pictures taken. I suppose there aren't many couples still together forty years after having a picture taken together during a senior photo shoot. God is so good.

"Commit your work to the LORD, and your plans will be established" (Proverbs 16:3).

38

I've been thinking about my relationship with Jesus. Having had it for as long as I can remember, I can take it for granted. But what made my faith unshakable and my relationship with Jesus the most important thing in my life? I needed him! In the hard times, when I went to dark places in my mind, when I felt alone and desperation was overwhelming, Jesus was all I had. And Jesus was all I needed. I learned to trust him. Pouring my heart to him in prayer was how I found rest.

If people know about Jesus but don't have a relationship with him, there may come a time in their life where something bad happens, and the person turns to Jesus to pray for help. Jesus celebrates when we turn to him! He anxiously awaits every person to seek him. He knows our needs before we ask. We have more needs than we may realize. Our specific prayer may not be answered the way we think it should be. God gave us all free will, and there is evil and illness in the world here on earth. Even Jesus can't control everything we wish he could. So we need to trust that he knows all of our needs and will help us, even when our prayers aren't answered the way we want them to be.

There's a song with the lyrics "some of God's greatest gifts are unanswered prayers." This is so true! Maybe a person will pray for the first time when they don't know what else to do. Even if their prayer isn't answered the way they want, God's desire is they'll recognize how their needs are being filled. Their heart opened the door to a relationship with Jesus. Jesus is there for us, no matter what happens, and he wants nothing more than to provide us everything we need, even if our prayer isn't answered how we had hoped.

God's greatest gift to us *is* Jesus. John 14:6 tells us "Jesus answered 'I am the way and the truth and the life. No one comes to the Father except through me.'" Not everybody knows about Jesus. Before Jesus died on the cross for the forgiveness of our sins, in Matthew 28:19–20, he commanded his disciples, "Therefore, go and make disciples of all the nations, baptizing them in the name of the Father and the Son and the Holy Spirit. Teach these new disciples to obey all the commands I have given you. And be sure of this: I am with you always, even to the end of the age."

It took me longer than it should have to become comfortable telling other people about Jesus, especially people who I don't know whether or not they know about Jesus. Trying to encourage people to know about Jesus and build a relationship with him is very important to me now. Every generation has their share of worries and problems to deal with. The world we live in right now is full of evil and cause for worry. Jesus was there for me. Jesus *is* there for all of us. We need to seek him in the hard times and also in the good times. We need to trust him and have faith he will provide for all of our needs. We can't walk away if our prayers aren't answered the way we want. We need to read his Word in the Bible and believe his promises.

I'm not much of an artist. My dad's best friend since childhood is, and as a child, I would watch him draw, and he would teach me how to draw. In an art class, I had an assignment to draw a face. I chose to try to draw the face of Jesus. It isn't great but certainly is the best piece of artwork I've ever created. It's amazing to me that no matter how big or small something I need is, Jesus always provides what I need when I choose him.

"Then Jesus said, 'Come to me, all of you who are weary and carry heavy burdens, and I will give you rest'" (Matthew 11:28 NLT).

39

The first year of college and commuting with my mom was when I started to recognize her ability to manipulate me. Anyone can manipulate others and not even realize they do it. I feel like alcoholics develop their skills to expert levels. Manipulation is a great way to try to cover up or make excuses for alcoholism. In my opinion, one of the symptoms of alcoholism should be when someone will not own their mistakes, problems, and hurting others.

Blame is one way to manipulate others. An alcoholic will blame everything on someone or something else. They seem unable to make the connection that what happened or how someone reacted actually started with the fact that they were drunk. Since my mom blamed me for everything for all of my teenage years, I carried the burden of a lot of guilt, even though I really wasn't to blame.

Being a victim is another way to manipulate others. An alcoholic will fixate on the "poor me" attitude to try to gain sympathy. When you love someone, you want to help them no matter how poor their excuses are. Life is hard for many reasons. It made me feel like a puppet being run with strings by her because I wanted her to stay out of trouble and not suffer the consequences that would result from her drinking. This is how I unknowingly became an enabler. I had to learn over time that it's best for everyone to stop enabling and let her suffer the consequences. Saying no and setting boundaries is tough love and extremely hard to do.

Anger is another way to manipulate others. To this day, if someone raises their voice, it gives me an adrenaline rush and makes me want to run away or crawl into a hole. Being angry and yelling is a form of coercion to get what he/she wants. I'd give in, just hoping the anger and yelling would stop. The ability to control anger is often lost when someone is drunk.

All of these ways to manipulate others and more is what I feel makes the emotional toll it takes on an alcoholic's loved ones unbearable. Years of emotional stress created issues for me that I've been dealing with since my teen years.

I developed the ability to manipulate others. I don't know if it's possible to be manipulated and not learn to do it. Years of repeat behavior creates habits. I guess the important thing is to recognize I can do it without realizing I'm doing it, so I need to be on guard to catch myself. Of course, I don't always accomplish this.

I've also struggled with anger. Certain things will trigger me into an anger that scares even myself. Through the years, I've learned to control it better, but I would guess that everyone in my family would say that I don't get angry very often, but when I do, you better look out. When my anger gets triggered, I get a huge adrenaline rush and I feel like I have to get it out of my body. Yelling and/or slamming doors or drawers was something I've done. That's not good. I've tried cleaning the house, pulling weeds, or shoveling snow to get it out. Hopefully, nobody triggers my anger to get me to do work now that I've disclosed this.

Being a victim is something I despise. I work really hard to take responsibility for my life. I could have chosen to be a victim, using the excuse that my mom verbally abused me and blamed me for her alcoholism. I could have felt sorry for myself, left my issues unaddressed, and do the minimum to get through life. Jesus was there for me. He doesn't want us to wallow in misery. God created each one of us with a meaningful purpose.

"For we are God's handiwork, created in Christ Jesus to do good works, which God prepared in advance for us to do" (Ephesians 2:10 NIV).

40

Graduation day came for Nate. His grad party would be the second time I met his huge family. His mom had fourteen siblings, and his dad had two. Then there were all the spouses and kids. It took years to remember all their names, and it's been awesome to be a part of such a large family.

The next step in our journey together was for Nate to start a one-year technical program at Control Data Institute, and I would complete my second and final year of college. Our plan was for Nate to move into our house so he, my mom, and me could all commute to work and school together. Looking back, I was an enabler and a caretaker in my family when I would have had the perfect opportunity to move away from home. And God bless Nate for moving into our house. He must have loved me a lot to do that and be the driver for our commutes with Mom.

And there was the fact that Nate and I didn't make enough money to have our own place while going to school full-time. So we made it work.

I had saved enough money for a down payment on my first car. My dad helped me get my first loan at the local bank. He cosigned but made it very clear he would not be making any of the payments. Together, we found a "stick shift" Chevy Monza. My dad bought me my own essential tool set and jumper cables. He told me I couldn't drive it until I could prove I could change the oil and change a tire with no help. I had always helped my dad in the garage. I was his tool fetcher. He taught me what all the tools were called, and it was my job to bring him the tools he needed when he needed them.

I was the one who did the driving hours with my brother when he took driver's education. I don't know what the current rules are, but back then, anyone over eighteen could do it. So we went driving all over in my car. I wanted to make sure we did all the things my dad had done with me when I learned how to drive, which included driving in some of the more tricky places to drive in the Twin Cities. My brother used my car to take his test to get his license. I did my best to be there for my brother and to take care of him the best I could.

A more recent definition of a caretaker is the role in the family that covers the addict's problems and responsibilities to try to keep everyone happy. It was a lot for me. So much to handle all at the same time. Jesus was there for me. I've learned it is impossible to make someone else happy. Happiness is something that needs to come from within. I had a lot of fears. But I kept focusing on the promise that I have nothing to fear when I choose him as the firm foundation for my life. If you're looking for a firm foundation on which to stand, Jesus is all we need and everything we need.

> Everyone then who hears these words of
> mine and does them will be like a wise man who
> built his house on the rock. And the rain fell, and
> the floods came, and the winds blew and beat
> on that house, but it did not fall, because it had

been founded on the rock. And everyone who hears these words of mine and does not do them will be like a foolish man who built his house on the sand. And the rain fell, and the floods came, and the winds blew and beat against that house, and it fell, and great was the fall of it. (Matthew 7:24–27)

41

Please forgive me if my struggle with control recurs throughout my book. I would like to control other people to behave the way I would like them to. Don't we all? How many of our daily emotional reactions are triggered by something someone else says or does? And then how many of those are undesirable emotions? Include not only your family members but everyone. With our "smart" phones, we can set up a non-stop stream of listening to people we don't even know trigger our emotional reactions.

Years of watching my mom destroying herself, one drink at time, made me want to control her behavior. And I mean a powerful desire. Imagine someone you love in a life-threatening situation, maybe like drowning. You would do anything in your power to save their life, correct? They want to survive, and you want them to survive. This would be minutes in time. Now imagine your desire to save them continuing for more than a decade. You are powerless, nobody can save them, and you're wondering if they want to survive or not. With every drink that nobody appears to be forcing them to drink, you want to save them.

Then add on the worry about them hurting or killing someone else. My mom was driving drunk daily. I was not going to give her rides to and from the bar. I worried about some poor innocent person or persons ending up in a car accident and maybe death because of her drunk driving. And I learned her level of drunkenness was getting to a point she would have fights in the bar with other alcoholics. I had to wonder, why on earth was anyone serving her alcohol at the bar anymore at all? So there I was, wanting to control the behavior of the bartender as well.

People who were concerned about my mom would tell me things about her. They thought I should know. And I appreciated it, but I still couldn't do anything to change anything about what she was doing. Alcohol was controlling her life to a point she was no longer in control of her life. As much as I wanted it, I certainly didn't have any control. It's a helpless feeling that started to consume me. I didn't want my mom to die so young. I prayed and prayed, but nothing could free her from the grip of alcoholism. The pain was almost unbearable, and I had suicidal thoughts because I didn't know how many years this would continue. The adrenaline is starting to rush through my body as I write this.

Back to Jesus for peace and rest that only he can provide. Jesus was there for me. He's there for all of us. I cannot even imagine going through what I did without Jesus. I really don't think I'd be here today. Without my faith and the ability to believe God's Word that Jesus will take our burdens, found in many places in the Bible, it would have been too much for me to handle.

We don't need to be a good person to build a relationship with Jesus. He meets us wherever we are. He knows we were born to sin. Without him, there would be no way for us to avoid God's judgment and eternal life in hell. There is no way to earn our way into heaven. That's why Jesus was born, crucified, buried, and rose again. We have the free gift of eternal life because Jesus died for all our sins. He doesn't want us to suffer. We all have free will and the power to make a choice about what we believe. I accept his grace, forgiveness, and gift of eternal life in a perfect heaven. While I'm still here, I remain a sinner but also want to tell you about Jesus. I hope you already have a relationship with him, but if you don't, please open your heart to him so you, too, can find peace and rest in a world that can make us weary.

"Cast all your anxiety on him because he cares for you" (1 Peter 5:7 NIV).

42

I wonder why and how people become alcoholics. Per the CDC, excessive alcohol use was responsible for more than 140,000 deaths in the US each year during 2015–2019 or more than 380 deaths per day. I don't think anyone sets a goal to become an alcoholic. It can "just happen," sometimes after decades of casual drinking. Something changes, and suddenly a drink is needed, and the alcohol takes control instead of the person who could control the alcohol.

When alcohol takes control, an endless battle begins. Those who "recover" still fight the battle every day to resist having a drink. These people have my utmost respect. My mom was the worst kind of alcoholic. She admitted she was an alcoholic, made it clear she wanted it that way, and told us to leave her alone. Experts say alcoholics have a "bottom" they need to hit before they will want to get the help they need to stop drinking. When we realized my mom's bottom was likely death, it's a feeling that can't be described with words. I couldn't make her want the help or want to stop drinking.

Maybe I'm biased, but I found it especially hard that it was my mother. Now maybe more so being a mother myself, it's so hard to imagine the power of alcohol being stronger than the innate power of a mother's love and desire to care for and help my children. Being verbally abused by my own mother through all of my teen years was damaging and painful, but as an adult, realizing my mom had no desire to survive her alcoholism was unbearable.

Unlike cancer and other terminal illnesses, alcoholism has the appearance of being a choice. She could choose to get the help she needed to stop drinking! Why was she choosing to kill herself one drink at a time? Why was she choosing to make alcohol her highest priority in life? There was so much more in her life! She had so many people who loved her, cared about her, would do anything to help her, and she didn't care. Her next drink was most important to her. This was my mom. I wanted to be important to my mom. This is how powerful the grip of alcoholism is. I knew my mom loved me, and I was important to her, but my mom was being drowned by alcohol and couldn't get back up for air.

Alcoholism is a thief. It steals all that's good from the alcoholic and steals the alcoholic from their family and friends. It's like the alcoholic is kidnapped and they're also the kidnapper. Treatment is available but not wanted or only works if the alcoholic wants it to work. Recovering from alcoholism is completely dependent upon the alcoholic wanting to recover. Nobody can make them want to recover. It's up to the alcoholic alone. This leaves everyone who loves them to fight their own battle of how to deal with it and learn to live with it. Watching someone you love die from something they had no choice in is hard. Watching someone you love die from something they do have a choice in is really hard.

God never promised life on earth would be easy. We live in a world filled with evil, Satan tirelessly tempting us to try to lure us away from God and eternal life in a perfect heaven. Our struggles can draw us closer to God and his glory or pull us deeper into the pain of evil destruction. Going through difficulty builds character, and we don't need to do it alone. Jesus was there for me. He's there for all of us. He went through immense suffering, even though he was perfect. He did it with purpose, providing a way to salvation for all of us.

"The thief comes only to steal and kill and destroy. I came that they may have life and have it abundantly" (John 10:10).

43

Spring and summer of 1984 was a time of significant changes.

When all of the love my dad had for my mom had been replaced with anger and resentment over time, he asked her to move out of our home and filed for divorce. I know his heart was completely broken. My mom moved to an apartment in town which was closer to the bars she frequented.

My brother got his license using my car to take his exam. I felt really good about having helped him accomplish that.

I graduated from Lakewood Community College, and Nate graduated from Control Data Institute. We had a big party at our farm. It was really fun with our friends and family there. My mom couldn't be there. She mailed a card to me with a letter that I have kept and read many times. I've even framed it and kept it near me on my desk at work. In her beautiful handwriting, she wrote the words I needed so desperately to hear.

JoAnn,

This note is between you and me. Please take it out of the card.

I'm with you all weekend in my heart. I just won't be there in person.

Well kid, we made it through "thick and thin" as Granpa used to say!

You deserve so much in life and knowing you, your goals will be set high and you will achieve them. Go for it!

I love you and remember I'm only a call way.

Love, Mom

I'm also very proud of you!

And in the card, she wrote, "May you always have what you want in life. You are very worthy of that. Love, Mom."

My mom lost her job. After several offers to have her position saved while she would get treatment covered by insurance, she declined, so her employer told her to leave too.

My dad, brother, Nate, and I were all living on the farm and working on the farm. Nate and I were seeking employment with unemployment rates around 7.5 percent. Back then, we had to walk into each company, resume in hand, and ask if there were any positions available for us to apply for. I was "pounding the pavement" in downtown St. Paul, and Nate had some leads in Bloomington. We both landed our first corporate jobs in July 1984. Nate's job required extensive travel in the five-state area and being on call.

Soon after, I moved to east St. Paul with a friend to be closer to work and ride the bus instead of driving and paying for parking.

Nate moved to west St. Paul with a guy he worked with and another guy. We dove in to the corporate IT world, living in the big city, and felt good about our big step toward building our future together.

My dad and brother stayed on the farm with my dad continuing to commute to east Minneapolis to work the afternoon shift. So my brother continued to be alone at night. I didn't feel bad leaving now that I knew the fighting between my parents was done and my brother was old enough to be alone. He may even have been a bit relieved that I was no longer "mothering" him.

Jesus was there for me. I found strength and peace to work hard, adjusting to being an adult living on my own and surviving on minimum wage. I started working out at a gym where I could get off the bus after work and then walk a couple of miles to my apartment when done. My friend and I often ate popcorn for dinner because it was all we could afford.

Although it was a huge relief to get out of the dysfunctional environment in the home where I grew up, I worried about my mom. She had now lost everything that everyone had tried to help her understand she would eventually lose. She lost her husband, daily interactions with her kids, her home, and her job. I knew what this meant. She would have more time and "reasons" to drink even more.

"Jesus Christ is the same yesterday and today and forever" (Hebrews 13:8).

44

Worry is defined as "to feel uneasy or concerned about something; be troubled" and "mental distress or agitation resulting from concern usually for something impending or anticipated." I worried about my mom a lot. She lived an hour away from me, alone, with no job and lots of time to drink. Calling her was "expensive" because it was long distance, so I didn't call her every day. And I visited her when I could. Mostly, I wrote letters to her and mailed them since there was no Internet or cell phones.

Without a job to do during the day, my mom started drinking all day every day for the most part. I could tell by the way she talked on the phone and when I'd visit on a weekend day it was clear she had already been drinking. She usually had a beer in her hand or sitting nearby. When I would visit, she didn't offer food like most moms. She didn't have much food on hand because she didn't eat very much.

She had always given her sister (my godmother) perms, even though she was never trained to do hair. And my mom had taught me how to give her perms. I continued to give her the perms she wanted, and she also asked me to cut her hair since she couldn't afford for someone else to do it anymore. So I gave it my best shot with her guidance. Her black hair flowed beautifully, so the cut didn't need to be perfect. Believe me, and my daughters will attest, I am not good with hair. My mom was never concerned about hairstyles, fashion, or having the best of anything. When she was sober, her love shined so beautifully that nobody would care about what she was wearing on the outside. Her beautiful face and blue eyes emitted the love she shared from her beautiful heart. I have tears flowing having written this because I miss her and her love every day. I wish you could look into her beautiful blue eyes.

I worried and worried. I feel like worry can be an unhealthy form of control. I couldn't control her or her drinking, but if I worried, then I felt like I didn't completely let go of the control I wanted. I continued to try to help her see she needed help to quit drinking or she would die. I continued to do research about alcoholism to better understand it and I looked for resources that could possibly help her. This was time-consuming without Internet.

She would tell me, "I'm fine. Don't worry about me." I was incapable of shutting off my worry. It was a heavy burden I carried with me. It sucked joy out of my joyful experiences because it took up space that would have been filled with only joy. I was always thinking about her and praying for her. I loved her so much. I loved the mother she used to be and wanted her back. But she remained locked up by alcohol, unable to escape, and seemingly sentenced to a slow torturous death.

Worry is usually temporary and will go away when the circumstance has passed. But what happens when the circumstance continues to last beyond a decade? It became more difficult for me to find peace. My prayers weren't being answered the way I wanted them answered. But Jesus was there for me. God's Word teaches us not to worry. We're human, and worrying is normal, but God doesn't want us to suffer because of worry. He wants us to trust he will provide what we need.

> But blessed are those who trust in the LORD and have made the Lord their hope and confidence. They are like trees planted along a riverbank, with roots that reach deep into the water. Such trees are not bothered by the heat or worried by long months of drought. Their leaves stay green, and they never stop producing fruit. (Jeremiah 17:7–8 NIV)

45

After my parents divorced, I felt like it was all on me to try to help my mom. Although Al-Anon was founded in the 1950s, I don't remember hearing about it then. I didn't know anyone or maybe just wasn't aware of anyone who was trying to help (or simply cope with) a loved one who was an alcoholic. Back then, without Internet and cell phones, people's lives were so much more private. We didn't talk as much about our problems. I felt alone in my struggles and worry about my mom.

I was just starting my adult life with dreams for the future while my mom was in her early forties and had gone full circle back to where she started, only worse. She should have been in her prime at that point. Instead, she was alone in an apartment, living on the money my dad had to pay her when their divorce settled, and her only goal seemed to be getting her next drink. I would talk with her when I visited. I told her I just didn't understand why and how she would continue with this lifestyle. What's there to like about it? I'd ask her if she wanted to have a future where she could enjoy grandkids and be a part of our family as it would grow. She'd say that, sure, she wanted that. When I'd ask her how she thought she would live long enough to enjoy it if she didn't make any changes, she'd shut me down and say she didn't need to make any changes. I'd ask her how I could help, and she'd tell me she didn't need any help. I'd present her with options I had found for resources that would be helpful. Again and again, she'd say, "I'm fine. Don't worry about me."

I told her I did worry about her. She was starting to look physically ill. Alcoholism was stealing her beauty and soul. It was as though her personality, love, and vigor for life were being snuffed out. I told her I loved her so much and was praying for her. I told her the greatest gift she could ever give me would be to stop drinking and take care of herself. She'd tell me she loved me too. I'd leave and start sobbing when I got in my car. How could she do this to herself? And, God, why aren't you answering my prayers for her?

Jesus was there for me. He's always there for you and me, never leaving us, even if we don't acknowledge his presence or spend time with him. At that time, I wasn't going to church and wasn't spending time reading the Bible. I wanted to control the circumstance and was determined to find a way to get her into treatment and stop drinking. Looking back, I wish I had been less like Martha and more like Mary in the story of Martha and Mary found in Luke 10. I spent much of my time like Martha, trying to do things and control things. I thought if I just try harder, do more, worry more, carry more that I'll get the outcome I wanted. My mom was the only one who could make the choices about her outcome. I had no control. Mary listened to Jesus as a priority, and she was less anxious and troubled. Jesus teaches us what is best for us. And in him we should put our trust.

> Now as they went on their way, Jesus entered a village. And a woman named Martha welcomed him into her house. And she had a sis-

ter called Mary, who sat at the Lord's feet and listened to his teaching. But Martha was distracted with much serving. And she went up to him and said, "Lord, do you not care that my sister has left me to serve alone? Tell her then to help me." But the Lord answered her, "Martha, Martha, you are anxious and troubled about many things, but one thing is necessary. Mary has chosen the good portion, which will not be taken away from her." (Luke 10:38–42)

46

It was hard to get ahold of my mom. We only had landline phones, and she rarely answered when I would call. It took some effort for me to not assume the worst when she didn't answer. She lived alone, so I had to hope that if something happened to her, somebody would call me somehow. I had a phone in my apartment and my own phone number at work, but if I wasn't near one of those, then I couldn't be reached by phone either.

My mom saved several of the letters and cards that I mailed to her. She saved everything related to my marriage to Nate. The first thing she saved was the letter I mailed to tell her that we were going to be engaged. I wrote:

Hi, Mom,

How are you doing? I'm doing just fine. I'm really happy too because Nate and I are going to be engaged! He came over to my apt on Wednesday to see me. He asked me if I wanted to go to La Belle's to look around for a while, so we went. When we walked into the store he told me we had to pick out my Christmas present and he walked straight to the diamonds. We looked in Ellsworth and River Falls on Sat. We're still trying to find just the right one. But I'll have it before Christmas. Nate's got just about enough cash saved for it. We won't get married for another couple of years. I hope you're happy for us! It's hard to get ahold of you so that's why I'm writing.

(I wrote a little more chitchat about my apartment and job.)

Mom, I hope you're taking good care of yourself. Remember I'll always love you—more than you know. See you later!

Love, JoAnn

I'm happy Nate knew me well enough to know that I wouldn't have wanted a surprise engagement with a ring that I didn't have input in choosing. He knew I liked to try to control things, and I'd be very picky about the right ring for me. We had fun, and I feel like the excitement lasted the whole time we spent looking at different rings at multiple places until we found just the right one.

I guess I don't remember if my mom wrote back, called, or waited until she saw me the next time to react to my news. I didn't save her letters and I don't remember for sure if she wrote letters to me. She didn't put much effort into having a relationship with me. It was pretty one-sided with me having to make the effort. And she probably had no idea how much energy I was burning worrying about her and trying to figure out how to help her.

I wondered what it would be like to have a mom who would have wanted to be involved in my happiness about our engagement and upcoming wedding preparations. By this time, I was accustomed to doing things on my own and starting to deal with the fact that our roles were reversed. Although I wasn't attending church or reading my Bible much, I knew I wasn't alone. Jesus was there for me. And he continued to put people in my life when I needed them. I had my relationship with Jesus, and that helped me stay strong and find peace.

I loved my mom and prayed for her. I didn't know what else to do. I tried to enjoy my life to the fullest. But the burden of my mom's alcoholism (note that I say her alcoholism, not her) was always there taking up energy I could have put toward my own responsibilities and goals. I was getting better at giving Jesus the burdens I couldn't carry, trusting the words in the Bible telling us to do that. I kept practicing "letting go and letting God" while I continued to want to control my mom's choices.

"For God alone, O my soul, wait in silence, for my hope is from him. He only is my rock and my salvation, my fortress; I shall not be shaken" (Psalm 62:5–6).

47

Once again, God put someone in my life when I needed her. I became friends with one of the women I worked with. She, too, had an alcoholic in her family and could understand where I was coming from. And she was recently engaged and starting to plan her wedding. It turned out that her wedding would be two weeks before mine. So for nearly two years, we did all kinds of wedding planning activities together. We were both in a situation where we'd be paying for our own weddings, so we were both interested in being thrifty in our planning and purchases for our weddings.

It's truly amazing to me how every step of my journey in this life, God provides for my needs. I believe with all my heart that this isn't just coincidence or luck. The strength and courage that comes from believing we don't need to get through this life on our own is unending. And God knows our every need, even when we don't.

Living away from my mom and with the direct verbal abuse from her ending, I thought I'd be just fine and go on with my life. I knew I still had the burden of worrying about her and trying everything I could do to help her. But I soon learned that I'd still go to dark places in my mind. This has never gone away fully. I have "triggers" that will lead me there. I'd say most often, it has been when I have been drinking but not always. Like so many others, my journey in this life has included a lot of learning about coping with the lasting impact of going through some traumatic things. We're only human with limited capabilities. And that's why I feel the strength that we can only get from faith in God is *so* important.

Satan is always at work. We can be tempted so much more easily when we are feeling weak and beaten down. Being a victim and blaming everything on something other than myself would have been the easier path. In this world, doing what's right and best for us is almost always the hard path and requires more effort. I refuse to be a victim. I want to take ownership of my life and fight hard to do better each day. Similar to how alcoholics are taught to take one day at a time, so too should everyone who is recovering from a trauma or an illness. Having faith that I'm not alone, that God will provide for my needs, and Jesus is there for me makes it much more achievable. Every morning, I can get up and put on the whole armor of God. So can you. Jesus was there for me, and he's there for you too, always and forever.

A final word: Be strong in the Lord and in his mighty power. Put on all of God's armor so that you will be able to stand firm against all strategies of the devil. For we are not fighting against flesh-and-blood enemies, but against evil rulers and authorities of the unseen world, against mighty powers in this dark world, and against evil spirits in the heavenly places.

Therefore, put on every piece of God's armor so you will be able to resist the enemy in the time of evil. Then after the battle you will still be standing firm. Stand your ground, putting on the belt of truth and the body armor of God's righteousness. For shoes, put on the peace that comes from the Good News so that you will be fully prepared. In addition to all of these, hold up the shield of faith to stop the fiery arrows of the devil. Put on salvation as your helmet, and take the sword of the Spirit, which is the word of God. Pray in the Spirit at all times and on every occasion. Stay alert and be persistent in your prayers for all believers everywhere. (Ephesians 6:10–18)

48

Life for my mom remained the same one day to the next. She lived alone and drank at home and at the bar. I'm not sure if she did much else. My brother and I would visit her, but it was painful to watch her sink further into alcoholism. When there were family gatherings, we'd make sure she made it there. Her family worried about her and would call or write and occasionally visit.

My dad met a woman and started a new relationship. My mom heard this, and she was upset about it. I'd listen to her complain and felt sad, too, that my parents' marriage had ended. It was like she was unable to make the connection that if she had stopped drinking, their relationship wouldn't have ended. Blaming everyone and everything other than herself is what alcoholics do.

I felt loss and sadness. I was years into feeling like I lost my mom. Even though she was still alive, we were losing her more every day. Our roles were reversed, and I was at a loss for more ways to try to help her. My parents' marriage had ended, and my dad was starting a new relationship with someone I wasn't too sure about. Our family unit was officially broken apart. But I cannot imagine how my mom felt. There was no way for me to comprehend what went through her mind, especially with alcohol in control.

At the same time I was anxious and excited about my future, I couldn't help but wonder how it would turn out. While we were busy planning our wedding, I wondered how long our marriage would last. My parents' marriage lasted twenty-two years with the last eight of those not great. Statistics showed I had a significant risk of becoming an alcoholic myself. Would we have children? I didn't think I wanted to have children. I felt exhausted of responsibility from doing my best to "mother" my brother since I was twelve and now "taking care of" my mom.

Nate and I didn't last very long in our separate residences in the big city of St. Paul. We grew up out in the country, and the change was a little much for us. Nate's roommates started having parties that included some drug use, so he wasn't comfortable living there. Nate was traveling a lot for his job and going to weeks-long training in Florida, so he wasn't there much but didn't want to be there at all. We started to search for a place to move in together in Hudson. We found a brand-new apartment building still being built and put ourselves on the list for renting an apartment as soon as it would be available.

Never a dull moment, Jesus was there for me. I think this was about the time when I realized I should pray for guidance instead of praying for what I wanted and what I thought was best. I started opening up my ways of thinking with my desire to control always there. Why did I think I knew what was best and making specific requests to God? I started to realize more and more that it was nothing but stressful to try to control much in life. I learned this over and over again. I was putting way too much pressure on myself to try to solve problems and make decisions for the future. The farther away

I was from the last time I had attended church or read the Bible, the more stressed I felt. Carrying my load and not giving at least some of it to God weighed me down. I needed to read my Bible and focus on God's promise to find peace, rest, and hope if I trust him more. I started to pray for wisdom, for God's will, and for his guidance.

"My child, eat honey, for it is good, and the honeycomb is sweet to the taste. In the same way, wisdom is sweet to your soul. If you find it, you will have a bright future, and your hopes will not be cut short" (Proverbs 24:13–14 NLT).

49

Grace and forgiveness are two of the most powerful gifts God gives us. While forgiveness is reactive, grace is proactive. While both can be very hard to do, they are what's best for the receiver and the giver. Without these, a person can carry around a growing load of unmet expectations, pain, and guilt. God gave us the gifts of grace and forgiveness so we can carry a lighter load. Jesus exemplified being the giver of grace and forgiveness and teaches us to do the same.

I like to think of grace as unconditional love toward a person who does not deserve it. In Christian terms, grace can be generally defined as "God's favor toward the unworthy." Romans 3:23 says, "For all have sinned and fall short of the glory of God." Forgiveness is to let go, release, or the dismissal of something. The two go together very well. Neither are easy but can free us from years of unnecessary suffering.

Forgiving my mom for the years of verbal abuse and blame took such a load off of me. It set me free of the anger I had built up. It was part of my process to "let go and let God." I hadn't thought about the benefits of forgiving someone else because until then, I thought the benefits were only received by the one forgiven. I, too, need forgiveness. We all sin and need forgiveness.

Grace would have been more difficult for me to give my mom if she wasn't my mom. I think there's an inherent unconditional love for your mom. Without forgiveness, I suppose it could be suppressed, but I never stopped loving my mom. Somewhere along the way, we started a tradition where we would say or write to each other, "Nobody's perfect, right?" I don't remember how that got started. And I always tried to remember that I need to separate my mom from my mom's alcoholism.

I tried to do things that would be positive for my mom. Even with all the hurt and burden of worry, she was my mom, and I loved her. I sent her a card that said "A special thank you for a special person" and wrote:

Mom,

I wanted to do something special to let you know how much I love you and appreciate all that you have done for me.

I always have appreciated all of the things you have done for me—but even just working the short time I have—I give you so much credit for not only working all of the years you have but also for raising my brother and I at the same time. I don't know how you did it but I give you all the credit in the world.

I really hope that you are happy now. I think it is best that you and Dad are apart. I guess you two just weren't meant to be together forever. I'm glad you were together long enough to give me life and a family I love very much. Even though we don't live together anymore, I love you more than ever! And don't worry, I'll never stay away from you or anything. I love to see you as much as I can. We should go out for supper soon! I love you, Mom!

Jesus was there for me. He's always there for you and me. Nobody's perfect, except Jesus. We can learn from him and do our best to love, give grace, and forgive others—even those who hurt us. We will find peace and the ability to go on one day at a time.

> Since God chose you to be the holy people he loves, you must clothe yourselves with tenderhearted mercy, kindness, humility, gentleness, and patience. Make allowance for each other's faults, and forgive anyone who offends you. Remember, the Lord forgave you, so you must forgive others. Above all, clothe yourselves with love, which binds us all together in perfect harmony. And let the peace that comes from Christ rule in your hearts. For as members of one body you are called to live in peace. And always be thankful. (Colossians 3:12–15 NLT)

50

As I'm writing this, I'm celebrating in my heart that on this day, sixty years ago, my parents were married. I have their wedding album and other special things from that day. And I framed my favorite photo from their album. The two of them are smiling, nose to nose, looking into one another's eyes, I'm guessing in the backseat of the car they left the church in. They look so happy and in love. They were beginning their married life together, not knowing what the future would hold.

In honor of my parents and the gift of life they created for me and my brother, I'd like to focus on love. The Bible is filled with teachings about love. God is love, and his love is perfect. We read "My command is this: Love each other as I have loved you" in John 15:12 (NIV). We are human and imperfect, so we do our best to love one another in an imperfect world with evil temptations, free will, and distractions.

The Bible teaches us about God's love for us, Jesus's love for us, and how we should love one another—even our enemies.

I once heard it is impossible to feel fear and love at the same time, that love is physically and non-physically the opposite of the fear/stress response. Our bodies are designed to live in love, not in fear. I find this so interesting. Science says so, and the Bible says so.

I wonder if this is the reason it is so incredibly confusing and painful to love an alcoholic. I feared my mom would die from alcoholism. I loved my mom unconditionally while hating her alcoholism. I knew she loved and believed in God, but she was unable to give up or escape the control of alcohol. I knew she loved me, but her alcoholism was running block and tackle on her ability to express her love. I have to believe she had fears, even though she didn't talk with me about them.

My parents loved one another so much. As my mom's alcoholism came creeping into their relationship, it hampered her ability to love my dad. My dad was hurt and angry that alcoholism was taking his wife away from him, and his love for her was slowly replaced with fear/stress. All the while, Jesus loved them. My brother and I loved them. We still had family love for one another and a shared love for Jesus.

I still cling to "love never fails," my life verse. Jesus was there for me. He was there for my parents, my brother, and for you—always. Jesus is love, and his love *never* fails. While our love isn't perfect and we do have fears, Jesus's love is perfect and unending. His love is unconditional, and he loves us in all of our imperfection. I believe the more imperfect we are, the more he seeks us out and loves us. His love is healing and ever-present for us to accept and find comfort in. As the children's worship song says, "Jesus loves me, this I know, for the Bible tells me so." Always know that.

> And so we know and rely on the love God
> has for us. God is love. Whoever lives in love lives
> in God, and God in them. This is how love is

made complete among us so that we will have confidence on the day of judgment: In this world we are like Jesus. There is no fear in love. But perfect love drives out fear, because fear has to do with punishment. The one who fears is not made perfect in love. (1 John 4:16–18 NIV)

51

Nate and I moved in to our new apartment in Hudson, just the two of us living together for the first time. With all the teaching about love and marriage in the Bible, I prayed for forgiveness of my sins. I wondered what my parents thought about it but didn't ask and don't remember them saying much about it. I feel like back then, living together before being married was frowned upon much more than now, but we weren't the only ones who made that choice.

Nate and I learned a lot about each other. My wedding planner friend and I talked a lot about what we were learning as she and her fiancé had moved in together as well. I remember us having a good laugh about why neither one of them could get their dirty socks into the laundry basket. The socks would literally make it within a foot of the laundry basket but not in the basket.

I started commuting to work with another gal I worked with. We'd take turns driving every other week. She was always really energetic in the morning and wanted to listen to Rod Stewart cranked up loud. We'd park in the cheapest lot we could find in St. Paul and walk almost a mile to our office building. One morning, she was extra energetic, so I asked her if she had drunk an extra cup of coffee or what was going on. As she was driving, she said, "Oh, I haven't slept for three days because I've been using cocaine."

Wait, what? I told her that I'll do the driving going forward and she should help pay for gas. Oh, my eyes were being opened up to a world much different than growing up on a farm near a small town.

The woman my dad started a relationship with moved in to our farmhouse with my dad and brother. With my dad working the afternoon shift in the Twin Cities, it left my brother home with her in the evenings. She started changing a lot of things in the house and yard, decorating with her preferred styles and making it her own. My brother didn't like living with her, so after a while, he decided to go live with Mom. I felt so bad for him.

My mom seemed happy to have my brother with her. It was hard for him to see the lifestyle she had, but he loved her unconditionally and accepted her the way she was. I wasn't able to do that. I always felt so determined to help her see that alcoholism was going to kill her if she didn't stop drinking. I found comfort knowing she wasn't there alone, but I felt bad for my brother.

Then my mom ended up in the hospital. Her colon had twisted, and she became very ill. Surgery was needed to remove part of her colon and put in a colostomy bag while her colon healed enough to be able to remove it (if it would). This scared my mom, so she "quit" drinking while she recovered. I'll never know if she quit completely or not, but it seemed she was motivated to recover quickly and fully. I spent much more time visiting and trying to help out by cleaning the apartment and making sure there was food to eat. I'd help her with her personal care as much as she wanted me to as well.

Jesus was there for me. He was there for all of us. I worried about her health, but it was sure nice to have her with a clearer mind. She had a sense of humor, even though it had to be awful to have a colostomy bag. My mom, brother, and I reconnected a bit. I let myself become very hopeful that this was her bottom and she would want to quit drinking, feel better, and have a better relationship with us instead of alcohol.

"Trust in the Lord with all your heart, and do not lean on your own understanding. In all your ways acknowledge him, and he will make straight your paths" (Proverbs 3:5–6).

52

My mom recovered, and they removed the colostomy bag. During recovery, her mind was more clear, and she told my brother and I that she wanted to quit drinking. She started looking for a job because the money my dad paid her when they divorced wouldn't last forever. And her will to entertain the desire to quit drinking didn't last either. Jesus was there for me.

She saved my card and letter:

Mom,

I'm very upset, I can't even work today. I'm just so very confused. Last night I called your place around 6:30 to find out how your interview went. I talked to my brother—he says you have drank every day last week except Thursday. Please don't be mad at him, you asked both of us to slap your hands when you drink. You know we are only trying to help you.

I know you must have drank Sunday before I even got there and I know you drank yesterday. I can tell the minute I hear your voice. It is a different tone when you drink and sometimes your words don't come out right. I know you are probably getting mad at me, but honestly Mom, I have to be honest with you—it doesn't help anybody to lie, or try to hide. You were doing so well there for a while. Now it seems you are making excuses and lying.

I realize it is hard to quit drinking, but please don't start using that as an excuse. I know you don't get totally drunk anymore, but still if you drink everyday it will be very easy for you to end up just like you used to be again. I don't know why you would want that to happen. You've already proved to yourself that you can quit for a few weeks, even under a lot of pressure. You keep saying how good you felt when you didn't drink, and how nice it was to not feel like a criminal.

Last night on the phone, I almost started to cry because I knew you had been drinking and yet you were telling me how awful drinking is and how it makes you lie. Please, Mom, don't pretend! I love you very much, but you've got to realize the more you drink and lie and try to fool me, a little bit of love and trust gets taken away. A few months ago, I thought it had all been taken away until you decided to quit. All can be forgiven and forgotten if you could just quit. I know it's hard and you're trying hard, but maybe you have to try harder.

You know you can make it at least a few weeks at a time, so why have you been drinking almost every day again? I would never make you do anything you don't want to, but you say you do want to quit. Words just aren't enough. If you need help to quit, there's nothing wrong with seeing a counselor. My brother and I would be glad to go with, but we won't force you into anything. I know you love me and my brother, but maybe just love is not enough.

I just know that right now, you've got a lot going for you. You have the will to quit, you know how good you feel when you quit, you've got total support from my brother and I, you've got your body all fixed up, you've got several good job prospects, and you've got half of your life to live yet. Please don't lose all of that to choose drinking instead! Take advantage of your strength to quit, I love you so very much when you don't drink. I want to help you!

I'm praying you'll get a job, I know that will help you. Please, try harder and harder! I pray God will give you the strength and will to quit.

You mean so very much to so many, please quit for you. I have faith in you.

Love, JoAnn

"Be strong, and let your heart take courage, all you who wait for the Lord!" (Psalm 31:24).

53

Nate continued to travel a lot for his job and going to Florida for weeks-long trainings. My best friend in high school would come to stay with me sometimes when he was gone for more than a week because I didn't like being home alone all the time. I really appreciated her company. She was to be my maid of honor in our wedding, so we spent time looking at bridesmaid dresses and other wedding things together.

In spring of the year Nate and I were getting married, we planned for me to join him in Clearwater, Florida, for a week, midway through a six-week training. It was the first time I flew on an airplane. Nate had to attend training on weekdays, but I was very content to lay by the pool all day. My mom saved the postcard I mailed to her.

Our wedding plans were coming along nicely. The woman my dad was with was skilled at making artificial flower bouquets and arrangements and offered to make all of them at cost. She had a nephew who did catering for a good price, so we went with him. Then she suggested her granddaughter should be my flower girl. I wasn't planning to have a flower girl and had barely met her granddaughter. We had decided to have a junior bridesmaid (the oldest girl in the family I babysat for so long) and a junior groomsman (one of Nate's nephews). She put a lot of pressure on me, so I agreed her granddaughter could be my flower girl. She was a little cutie.

Then she insisted that my dad and her be married before our wedding. She said something about it not being right for them to be unmarried as parents of the bride. They had known each other less than two years. I didn't understand at all why suddenly this became important. But now another wedding was being planned, and their wedding date was set to be a month before our wedding. I didn't like this at all. If my brother didn't want to live with her and now this, I was even more uncertain if she would be good for my dad and us.

I had a unique concern to address for my wedding. I needed to make plans for how to handle the risk that my mom would get drunk and cause a scene at some point throughout our wedding, dinner, and dance. She had told me herself that her drinking had resulted in screaming and even physical fights. I knew she was upset about my dad having a new relationship and now a new marriage. She had proven time and time again that her promise to not drink would be broken. The last thing I wanted to happen on our special day was for my mom to cause a scene with no plan to deal with it.

I reached out to two of my cousins, both her nephews and god-sons. I asked them to keep an eye on her and, if she started causing a scene, to please escort her out as peacefully as possible. They understood my concern and agreed. I remember feeling just awful telling my mom that. I loved her so much and wanted her to enjoy every minute of our wedding day with us. I asked her to please not drink that day. And I told her the plan for how it would be dealt with if she did.

Setting boundaries is hard. I've learned it's okay to set boundaries to protect ourselves. We all have limits on our capacity to deal with issues. What we're dealing with just in ourselves may be more than we feel like we can handle. Layering on top the issues of others can easily take away the energy we need to handle our own. It is *okay* to set boundaries with other people regarding how much you can let their issues impact you.

Jesus was there for me. I prayed for guidance and peace as I tried to navigate life and focus on the good.

"Continue steadfastly in prayer, being watchful in it with thanksgiving" (Colossians 4:2).

54

"I didn't drink." "I won't drink." Are these lies, goals, or simply what an alcoholic thinks their loved one wants to hear? For me, it's like torture or at least a lasting emotional turmoil.

For most of the first decade of my mom's alcoholism, she had made it very clear that she had no intention of trying to stop drinking. I feel like I went through a decade of mourning as I was losing my mom. I don't remember feeling hope she might recover from her alcoholism. Because she chose me as her "scapegoat," I endured almost daily verbal abuse that my brother describes as vulgar.

I've already shared about most of this and how I went to dark places in my mind while trying to process all of my emotions. I have no doubt that I would not be here today if I hadn't had an ever-growing faith in Jesus Christ. I believe the words in the Bible that Jesus loves us and will take our burdens if we let him. I felt I had no choice, really. I could let the pain and burden I felt lead me to acting on my suicidal thoughts or trust that I could give what I couldn't handle to Jesus. Jesus was there for me. My faith enabled me to ease the load I carried and the pain I felt.

I often think of the words in the "Footprints in the Sand" poem, when the Lord whispered:

My precious child, I love you and will never leave you
Never, ever, during your trials and testings.
When you saw only one set of footprints,
It was then that I carried you.

All of the things I learned through the first phase of my mom's alcoholism continued to help me as we moved into the next phase. With my mom's illness, surgery, and recovery, we shifted into a new phase where she told us she didn't drink or won't drink. This brought hope. Somehow I still had an inherent trust in my mom. And so began the roller coaster of promises and hope, hearing what I wanted to hear so badly, and being let down over and over again. Trusting an alcoholic is like playing with fire. I would get close to feeling like I could trust her saying she didn't want to drink and then get burned again. Looking back, I think I feel this phase was worse than the first. It was kind of like a never-ending game of Russian Roulette. Alcoholism is another game of lethal chance.

Will my loved one die from alcoholism? She could make the choice to stop drinking with all the resources available to help and support her. Why won't she make that choice and stick with it? There are people with terminal illnesses fighting for their lives, going through horrible treatments and doing everything they can to live. They have terminal illnesses where they don't have a choice. They fight because they want to be there for their family. Mom, why won't you make the choice to stop killing yourself with alcoholism and be there for us? How long will I be able to love you enough to continue to try to help you realize what you're doing? How do I go about living my own life while I'm consumed with worry and stress about what you are and are not doing?

And still Jesus was there for me. My mom had free will to make decisions for her. I, too, had free will to make decisions for me. Jesus was there for both of us. Love is powerful and love never fails. Jesus *is* love. Without him, I either wouldn't be here or I wouldn't be who I am. I'm imperfect, just the way God made me. Jesus loves us and accepts us no matter how we are or what we've done. He gives us grace, forgiveness, and an unconditional offer for everlasting life with him in paradise. Accept it.

"And the Word became flesh and dwelt among us, and we have seen his glory, glory as of the only Son from the Father, full of grace and truth" (John 1:14).

55

While on the roller coaster of lies and disappointments, I drove myself crazy trying everything I could to help my mom. I tried positive reinforcement and tough love. I tried to trust her and have faith in her to do the right thing. There's only one human (or once human) I can truly trust and have faith in, and his name is Jesus Christ. Jesus was there for me. All other humans, including myself, are imperfect and have the potential to let us down. Although imperfect, God blesses us with many who love us, do their very best to be trustworthy, and hold us up when we need them.

Nobody thinks they'll become an alcoholic. It starts with casual drinking with the person in control. For some people, not sure why or how, it's like a flip of a switch, and suddenly, the alcohol is in control. The length of time it takes for the transition from the person drinking being in control to the alcohol being in control varies person to person. God made us capable of adapting to change. The alcoholic adapts to alcoholism, and their loved ones adapt to them becoming an alcoholic, most of the time without noticing until bad things begin happening as a result.

As the struggle continued, this is one of the letters I wrote to my mom that she saved (page 1 of 2):

Dear Mom,

I'm writing this letter because I don't know what else to do. Please let me explain.

For the past ten years I have been watching you hurt yourself. Now, I realize your life has not been easy and the older I get the more I know that. But please don't keep thinking about all of those bad things. There is a great future for you to look forward to. Don't take that away from yourself too. Whether you want to believe it or not, the vast majority of your problems in the last five years were caused by a disease called alcoholism.

It have been a very slow developing disease with you which you hid well at first. But that disease cannot be hidden forever because it continues to get worse. I am certainly no expert on alcoholism but I have learned all I care to from you. It's not your fault that you got it. It has a way of sneaking up on people without them knowing what's really happening. I'm sorry to say, but I know a lot more about you and what's been happening with you than you probably think. The reason for this being that people who know you and care about you tell me what they see and ask me why you're letting what's happening happen.

Everybody knows you have a drinking problem and would be very supportive to you in overcoming it, but you have to want to. Here's my position: I love you and care about you deeply. Right now I consider things to be bad enough that I have to do something soon or you won't be around anymore. You've got so much to live for, why do you want to throw it away? You're very intelligent, beautiful and young—why ruin it? How can I convince you that you don't need beer to be happy? You don't need it for anything do you? Is it really fun to get so drunk that you hurt yourself? Why do you think you bruise so easy? Your blood vessels are thinner from having alcohol in them all the time.

Don't you feel awful? Try to remember how it felt to be strong and healthy, not shaking and controlled by beer. You can overcome it, I know you can! There are many people who would do everything possible to support you and be with you including myself, your son, your sisters, Nate and many others. What will it take to convince you that you have a problem and desperately need help? So far, you've lost your husband and home (maybe you didn't want it anyway) and your job. You've gotten a DWI and have had other problems with cops. How much more is there to lose but your life?

56

One of the letters to my mom that she saved (page 2 of 2):

If people don't talk to you like they used to, it's because it hurts them to see you hurt yourself and what they really want to do is shake you and tell you to get out of Spring Valley and away from a beer can. Or they want to hug you and tell you that everything will be okay if you just quit drinking. They just don't have the heart. Now you may think I'm lying but I have people who care about you tell me this quite often. Everybody is concerned about you Mom! Grandpa used to ask me if you were still drinking when I'd go to see him. He knew you had a problem too, but it hurt too much for him to confront you with it. A lot of people are carrying a burden because they are so worried about you. I just thought you should know that. Everybody tells me that you're so lucky to have a daughter who hangs in there, still loves you and keeps faith in you. It would be so much easier to take the attitude that if you don't care about yourself then why should I care either. But I do care! If you're so lucky to have me, then why did you choose sitting at the bar at 11 am over coming home to talk with me a little?

Mom, I have always loved you and always will. But I want you to know that it hurts to love someone who doesn't appear to care about themselves. Sometimes the hurt is able to overcome the love. That shouldn't be the way it has to be. I am begging you, please get help to overcome your alcoholism. I promise I'll be at your side to help you. Whatever you need, just say so. I'm begging you! Can't you see you have real friends who really care? Can you honestly call the people in the bar your friends? They don't care about you do they? If they do, why do they punch you, call you names, and continue to buy your drinks when they know eventually that those will be the drinks that will kill you? Please Mom, call someone who loves you and cares about you and let's all help you to get well!! Just in case you would like to talk to someone about your problem who doesn't know you, here is a number to call: xxx-xxx-xxxx. It's a number to Care Unit in Golden Valley, a 24-hour counselor. I think I will call that number myself to get some counseling. It is getting harder and harder for me to cope with the hurt of seeing you hurt yourself.

I LOVE YOU, please do something to help yourself quit drinking. Don't you want to live to keep getting flowers, to see your kids get married, to see your grandchildren? You deserve it. Don't let alcoholism rob you of anything else PLEASE!

With all my love, JoAnn

There are no words to describe the helplessness, frustration, anger, and pain I felt every day. Watching someone you love slowly die is one of the hardest things to do. Watching someone you love slowly die because they won't stop drinking the thing that's killing them is really tough. There's a "cure," but the next drink was always more important. It was more important than being home when I came to visit. It was more important than everything else in life for her. My role shifted from being her scapegoat to being the single point of contact for everyone who wanted to report something about her or ask something about her. And I felt solely responsible to be the one who had to convince her to get help to save herself with no legal way to force her.

Jesus was there for me. I had to believe the promises written in the Bible that Jesus would take my burdens, give me strength, keep me sane, heal my pain, give me peace, and grant me wisdom.

"I can do all things through him who strengthens me" (Philippians 4:13).

57

I believe in God and the Holy Spirit. I believe in Jesus Christ, my Lord and Savior. I believe he died for the forgiveness of my sins, was buried, and rose again. I believe I'll have everlasting life in heaven. But how can I believe this and why?

Who do you believe and why? Do you believe people you've never met? Someone on the news? Someone with their own blog? Someone on social media? Someone who wrote a book? How about *Wikipedia*?

Do you believe life is a series of choices and consequences that just happen and some people are lucky and some are not? Do you feel alone and overwhelmed by life? Do you wonder why bad things happen to you while others seem to skate through life without bad things happening to them?

Do you feel like you have intuition? Do you trust your intuition? Do you feel weak or strong? Do you have a purpose? Who do you trust and why? Who do you have a relationship with and why? Who in your life has always been there for you and never let you down? What or who sustains you?

Is your body and mind a miracle? Who designed our bodies and how did we come to be? Watch a baby be born and grow. Look at the earth we live on and the beauty of life we see in plants and animals.

Look at the skies with clouds and stars. Is this all created by a God who loves us or did it all just happen somehow?

Do you know what will happen to you when you die? Do you think you'll disappear forever into nothingness? Is there some alternative universe where you'll go? Do you think there's heaven and hell and you'll be judged as to which one you'll go? Will you know anybody where you go? Will you forever be alone?

Do you believe the outcomes from many people researching and studying something for many years? I have read the entire Bible. The Bible was written by many people over more than a thousand years. It includes prophecy and witness accounts. Although the books of the Bible are written by different people at different times, there is consistency. The Bible has been translated and some say that's why we shouldn't believe it. I say if you haven't ever read the entire Bible, save your judgment until you have.

What if I'm wrong and I'm believing in something that isn't real? What if you're wrong and believing in something that isn't real? What if the Bible is correct, and there is only heaven or hell when you die? What if you don't believe that and you end up in hell when you die? The Bible describes hell as darkness, gnashing of teeth (suffering), unquenchable fire, and separation from God. Why risk that?

Not only is there a promise of hope after we die, there is promise of hope while we live here on earth. I am so much more because I have a relationship with Jesus Christ. I find strength, peace, discernment, grace, forgiveness, love, patience, perseverance, really everything I need. When I trust him and stop trying to control things in my life, my life goes much better. I really don't know what to think or what to do, but he does. If I felt alone without Jesus, I wouldn't be able to get out of bed to face each day. There's so much evil, and Satan wants to lure every one of us to evil and eternal damnation in hell.

Jesus was there for me. He's always there for me and for you. Please believe in him. He died on a cross for the forgiveness of our sins while he was sinless. He rose from the grave to glory. We need to believe in him, accept him as our Savior, and accept his gift of eternal life. While here, I want to try my best to tell everyone about Jesus and pray for more people to grow a relationship with him.

"Let love be genuine. Abhor what is evil; hold fast to what is good" (Romans 12:9).

58

I kept on doing my best to help my mom while trying to live my life too. I find it interesting to read the letters I wrote to her that she had decided to save. They're more than thirty-five years old now, and I can hold them in my hand, just like she did. I wonder why or how often she would read them. In the digital age now, I wonder how many memories will be lost forever in "the cloud." I'm grateful to have the letters now.

This was one I had written with hope after a morning visit. I started limiting my visits to morning because I felt like it was a waste of time to try to visit at other times of the day.

Mom,

How are you doing? I just want to let you know it was so nice to see you, and even more nice to see you drinking coffee instead of beer. Mom, it is so much nicer to hug you and love you when you aren't drunk and don't smell of smoke and alcohol. I have been thinking a lot lately of all the nice characteristics you have when you're not drinking. Please quit drinking for good so you can be the wonderful person you are when beer is not controlling you.

Mom, I know it would be hard for you to totally quit by yourself, and I want you to know I am more than willing to go with you to someone we can talk about alcoholism with so we both understand what it does and how it affects us. I know in my heart you can overcome alcoholism. I have been praying you will for years.

The first step is to decide you want to. You are strong and smart and I know that together we can fight this illness. This would be the first step in being successful in finding and keeping a good job. I would really love it if you could move close to Hudson, even with me or your sister for a while. We can have supper together, and do all kinds of fun things. If you would get a job in St. Paul, we could carpool together.

I've been checking on places where they help people overcome alcoholism. There are a lot of outpatient types of programs where you could stay with me (or wherever you want) and I could go with you to help you be your good self again.

I promise to help you, Mom. I love you too much to ignore your problems any more. I want to help, will you let me? Promise me we can talk about this soon.

Love always, JoAnn

Sorry this paper is yucky, but "nobody's perfect," right?

I wish I could remember how we got started with saying to one another "nobody's perfect." How appropriate and what a powerful reminder of the grace and forgiveness we're offered. We were created to be imperfect. Jesus is the only human, ever and always, who was and is perfect. He is the son of God, born of a virgin, tempted by evil like all of us, suffered pain, and experienced everything we do. He did not sin. We do. We all sin in our thoughts and deeds. We are imperfect by design, born with free will. Jesus was there for me and always there for all of us. He yearns for a relationship with each and every one of us.

But now the righteousness of God has been manifested apart from the law, although the Law and the Prophets bear witness to it—the righteousness of God through faith in Jesus Christ for all who believe. For there is no distinction: for all have sinned and fall short of the glory of God, and are justified by his grace as a gift, through the redemption that is in Christ Jesus, whom God put forward as a propitiation by his blood, to be received by faith. This was to show God's righteousness, because in his divine forbearance he had passed over former sins. (Romans 3:21–25)

59

Our wedding plans were coming along nicely. We were busy with jobs, Nate's training trips, and me trying to help my mom. I'm not sure why, but I chose this time to cut my hair short for the very first time. Nate loved my long hair, but I guess I just felt like I needed a change. We had our engagement photos taken and made all of the traditional announcements of our upcoming wedding.

As with most relationships, we both came with our own brokenness and unresolved issues. We had our share of arguments. I was stressed out all the time, even though I tried not to be. Being apart so much was hard. Nate traveled for his daily work and had to travel to Florida for training for weeks and weeks. I had to say no when I'd get phone calls from my mom late at night for things like asking me to drive her back to a bar forty miles from my apartment because she forgot her purse there. Life on this earth is hard, right? It's not heaven.

We had twelve weddings the year we were married, and ours was the last. Nate and I were in four of them. Not only was it a very busy year, it was expensive! We must have really scrimped to get by and pay for a year full of wedding attire and gifts. Bachelor and bachelorette parties galore too. I'm grateful it wasn't a thing back then to take trips for the bachelor and bachelorette parties. Looking back, I'm really not sure how we did all of that!

We had so much more to learn. At the time of our wedding, I was twenty-two, and Nate was a month away from his twenty-second birthday. God brought us together as just kids, knowing more about what we needed than we did. There's been times when I didn't like Nate, didn't like the things he did or the things he said, and I'm sure he can say the same. But our love for one another has endured. Jesus was there for us. We believe in Jesus Christ and do our best to live life based in love, absolutely imperfect but trying our best to do good.

If I speak in the tongues of men and of angels, but have not love, I am a noisy gong or a clanging cymbal. And if I have prophetic powers, and understand all mysteries and all knowledge, and if I have all faith, so as to remove mountains, but have not love, I am nothing. If I give away all I have, and if I deliver up my body to be burned, but have not love, I gain nothing.

Love is patient and kind; love does not envy or boast; it is not arrogant or rude. It does not insist on its own way; it is not irritable or resentful, it does not rejoice at wrongdoing, but rejoices with the truth. Love bears all things, believes all things, hopes all things, endures all things.

Love never ends. As for prophecies, they will pass away; as for tongues, they will cease; as for knowledge, it will pass away. For we know in part and we prophesy in part, but when the perfect comes, the partial will pass away. When I was a child, I spoke like a child, I thought like a child, I reasoned like a child. When I became a man, I gave up childish ways. For now we see in a mirror dimly, but then face to face. Now I know in part; then I shall know fully, even as I have been fully known.

So now faith, hope, and love abide, these three; but the greatest of these is love. (1 Corinthians 13:1–13)

60

Our big day came, and everything went perfectly, except my personal attendant who did my hair and makeup accidentally burned my forehead with the curling iron. Oh my goodness, she felt just horrible. I told her to just cover it up with more makeup.

Over four hundred people came to celebrate our marriage. We had the time of our lives! Nate still says, "Your wedding day is one of only two days when everyone will gather to celebrate you but the only one where you'll be alive to enjoy it." So true. When we had a moment to reflect on the day for the first time, we both cried tears of joy and appreciation for everyone who loves us.

We had our wedding at the church. I'll always remember the pride and love I felt from my dad as he walked me down the aisle. We couldn't gain agreement from my parents to get a photo with both of them in it together or a family photo with all of my family together. My dad's new wife had to be in the photos with my dad. It turned out their marriage was short, so I'm grateful I have one photo of just my dad and I.

I had found a marriage prayer. We asked everyone attending to pray for us during our ceremony.

Lord, help Nate and JoAnn to remember
when they first met, and the strong love that grew

between them. To see the good within the other, and find answers to all their problems. Help them to say the kind and loving words, and make them big enough to ask forgiveness of the other. We put their marriage into your hands. Amen.

Jesus was there for us. What an incredible feeling to have a church full of our closest family and friends praying for us and our marriage! And God has been the strong third cord in our marriage, holding us together all of these years. A threefold cord is not quickly broken. We all need each other and we all need God. We were created for fellowship.

Our dinner and dance was at Proch's Ballroom. We had a live band called Rainbow Eyes. Everyone danced and danced. We were a sweaty mess. At one point, someone stepped on the train of my dress as I was dancing away, and the whole train ripped away, exposing my undies. My bridesmaids and personal attendant came running to me. With a box of safety pins, they managed to get it secured again. Everyone was having so much fun. When the band was quitting for the night, we took a collection and asked them to play another half hour (still not enough). The place was still full, and nobody wanted to stop having fun. We closed down the place.

My mom didn't drink, so she didn't need to be escorted out by my cousins (her godsons). I was so grateful! Of all the days in my life I really needed her to be my mom without alcohol, that surely was one. It was the greatest gift she could have given me.

It was an unforgettable day and celebration full of love and joy, followed by a lovely honeymoon to Estero Island, Florida. We were truly blessed as we began our life as husband and wife.

> Two are better than one, because they have a good reward for their toil. For if they fall, one will lift up his fellow. But woe to him who is alone when he falls and has not another to lift him up! Again, if two lie together, they keep warm, but how can one keep warm alone? And though a man might prevail against one who is alone, two will withstand him—a threefold cord is not quickly broken. (Ecclesiastes 4:9–12)

61

A good friend asked me a question I've always wondered about myself. Why isn't love enough for an alcoholic to stop drinking? I don't think I'll ever know the answer to that question. Our love surely isn't perfect, but Jesus's love is. Jesus loves every person, but for some, it still isn't enough to desire a relationship with Jesus. It makes me think that love must be received by the person it is given to or it is easily missed or ignored. Maybe the grip of alcohol is powerful enough for the alcoholic to be completely blind to the love given to them or emotionally unable to receive it. Maybe alcohol can bring the alcoholic to a level of depression where they cannot feel the love given to them.

My mom told me that alcohol was the first and foremost thing on her mind. From what I've researched, alcoholics don't truly love alcohol. It's more of a codependent relationship in which they cannot leave but kills them to stay. An alcoholic will defend their relationship with alcohol when anyone threatens it, even until death. It was evident to me my mom wasn't capable of loving herself because of her alcoholism. And it made her self-centered and lose sight of what we needed from her.

My mom had an incredibly strong faith but she had written that alcohol was even pulling her away from it. I picture Jesus holding on to her as tight as she would allow him to. I believe that she never strayed away completely, but I think her alcoholism made her numb to feeling love from Jesus as well. I don't think a person who has not been in the firm grip of alcoholism could ever understand the power it has. So while there's so much I don't understand about my mom as an alcoholic, I pray I never understand it. I focused on the love she gave me prior to the alcoholism as well as all of the glimpses of her without alcohol that would still be there at times while she was an alcoholic.

I wrote a thank-you note to her following our wedding that she saved. It read:

Mom,

Thank you so much for the very generous gift of money and the TV trays. We're using them now! Special thank you Mom for not drinking on our special day. That made our day absolutely perfect! We enjoy seeing you sober so very much. You're an absolutely lovely person and we love you very much!

JoAnn & Nate

Do you have people in your life that aren't fun to give gifts? The ones who open a gift and while you're expecting their reaction to be one of pure joy, there's nothing? Maybe you're left wondering if they don't like the gift but don't want to hurt your feelings. Or maybe it's that they don't feel like they deserve it. You don't really know why, but it seems almost difficult for them to accept the gift.

I wonder if this is how Jesus feels when we are unable or choose not to feel his love and/or choose not to accept him as our Savior. He loves every one of us completely and perfectly. Jesus was there for me. He's always there for me and for you. He died on the cross, rose to life again from the grave, and offers us forgiveness of all of our sins and eternal life in heaven. Please receive his love and accept his gift of eternal life.

> No, in all these things we are more than conquerors through him who loved us. For I am sure that neither death nor life, nor angels nor rulers, nor things present nor things to come, nor powers, nor height nor depth, nor anything else in all creation, will be able to separate us from the love of God in Christ Jesus our Lord. (Romans 8:37–39)

62

My mom had started spending time with a man named Al. I don't know exactly what their relationship was for sure. But I do know Al was good to my mom, and I'm grateful she had someone who cared about her. He clearly accepted her as she was and could see through the alcoholism to the beautiful person trapped inside. He attended our wedding with her and, I believe, supported her in my wishes for her not to drink at our wedding. He didn't insist on being in our family photos and instead beamed with joy for my mom being the mother of the bride.

Mom's life seemed so simple and yet so complex. She worried about making enough money to pay her bills (and have an adequate supply of alcohol). She was able to gain employment through a temp agency, but most jobs didn't last long for obvious reasons. Having worked from a young age and making good money in her prime, I know it really bothered her to not have a steady job, and she worried a lot about not having enough money.

As hard as it was for me, I continued to visit her, cut and permed her hair, and tried to do and say things that would build her up. At the same time, I was trying everything I could think of to try to help her see she needed help to stop drinking. She was not only mentally and emotionally addicted to alcohol; she was now physically addicted. I don't know or maybe don't remember if anyone else was trying to confront her about her alcoholism. I know I felt alone in the effort.

I loved her so much, but I would get so angry when I'd get a call from her wanting my help because she was drunk. I would feel so hurt and betrayed when I'd arrange for a visit only to find her not home because she was already at the bar. I'd get so frustrated when she'd already be drinking again in the morning when I would visit. It was always the alcohol. I just desperately wanted my mom without the alcohol.

I started a journey of seeking a way to commit her to treatment. I set up meetings with the police, then an attorney, and even a judge. I got the same response from all of them. Legally, I could not commit her to treatment. She had to make the decision for herself. I could seek a seventy-two-hour hold and hope she would make the decision to get the inpatient treatment she needed. I felt so helpless and angry! How would my mom's mind possibly clear enough in that short of a period of time to realize she needed treatment to save her life? Why won't you let me help her? She doesn't know she needs the help! What am I supposed to do? Just watch her kill herself for however long it takes?

I imagine it must have been difficult for the people I consulted with to need to tell me that was all I could do. I'm not good at having a poker face, and I'm sure all of my emotions were clearly visible in my face. The law made no sense to me. If someone has a gun to their head or has slit their wrists, I could call for help and get it. But if my mom is killing herself by drinking alcohol all day, every day, I needed to just helplessly watch and deal with all of the stress it brought to my daily life. Nothing about this made any sense to me!

Jesus was there for me. Not all of the teaching in the Bible is about what we should seek to receive but rather is about how we should love and what we should give.

"But if anyone does not provide for his relatives, and especially for members of his household, he has denied the faith and is worse than an unbeliever" (1 Timothy 5:8).

63

As I write this, I feel such heavy sadness. Today, September 26, marks another year since the day my mom died. I always feel such sadness, even though so much time has passed. I think about everything she has missed that alcoholism robbed from her. I guess yesterday was National Daughter's Day. Having two daughters of my own now, I feel every day is Daughter's Day. I love them more than I thought was possible to love someone. My mom didn't get to meet them. But I can tell you I felt her love, strength, and presence while I was in labor and delivery with both of them.

I'll share a story, and you can think what you want. One day, I was driving with our girls in the back seat. They were just old enough for both of them to talk. I remember exactly where we were when this happened. They chitchatted or sang all the time in the car. All of a sudden, they started talking about Grandma Judy (my mom). I hadn't talked about my mom with them, assuming they were too young to understand about a grandma they couldn't see. I just about had to stop the car. I was so bewildered listening to them talk about my mom. It really makes me wonder about what young children's minds, not yet conditioned to have limitations, can comprehend.

It's been very difficult for me to live life without my mom. I try hard to be there for our girls as they raise their children. Oh, what

I would have given for my mom to have been there for me. I think about all of the joy I have while spending time with my grandkids and think about all of the special moments my mom didn't get to enjoy. There's been times I feel angry that I was robbed of having my mom, and she was robbed of all that she has missed.

Jesus was there for me. He's there for me today as I cry tears again because I miss my mom. I give her the credit for planting the seed of faith in me. She gave me a firm foundation by teaching me, praying with me, and nurturing me while I grew a relationship with Jesus when I was young. Without it, I would not have made it through the traumatic things in my life. Faith is such a difficult thing to explain to someone who isn't sure how to have it.

God gives us new hope every day. I'm so grateful for every day I live beyond the age my mom did. I feel an extra sense of appreciation for every moment I spend with my beautiful family. I'm grateful my mom was freed from the prison of alcohol that held her captive. Her suffering came to an end, and I have blessed assurance she is at peace and happy in her forever heavenly home. I also believe I'll be reunited with her when my time comes to pass. I'm committed to be my best and do my best to seek God's guidance and do his will.

I feel like the most difficult times in our lives are when we grow the most. When life is hard, we tend to seek and rely on God more. There's a saying that goes something like "We know God is enough only when he's all we have." If you've never felt that way, I pray you never do. It's a difficult place to be when you're so down that you feel like God is all you have. But, truly, God is all we need. He gave us Jesus and all things we have in our lives. He blesses those who love him and will provide for our every need. He seeks out those who still need him and don't know it yet. He wants each of us to help others find him and grow a relationship with him. I pray you do.

"Yet what we suffer now is nothing compared to the glory he will reveal to us later" (Romans 8:18 NLT).

64

Since learning I really had no hope of being able to commit my mom to treatment for alcoholism, I felt so scared. I started thinking about what would happen as her disease progressed further. I researched it, and it sounded like a horrible way to die if in the end she would die as a direct result of alcoholism. Upon advice from the attorney and judge who had graciously met with me, I would need to prove she was a threat to herself or others in order to put a seventy-two-hour hold on her. I didn't know how I would do that, and based on how things had gone already, I was pretty sure she would leave after seventy-two hours. The only other way she could get a seventy-two-hour hold would be if an incident would happen where the cops would deem it necessary. Given the fights she told me about getting into, perhaps there was a chance that would happen.

What twenty-two-year-old wants to need to think about all of that? I was the kid, and she was the parent, but it sure didn't feel that way. I wanted to be living carefree and having fun. And I still did. I tried to do it all. Looking back, I don't know how I did everything I had on my plate at that time with the emotional toll it was taking on me. Jesus was there for me. Without the love, strength, and peace I found in Jesus, I know I couldn't have made it through it all. In my relationship with Jesus, I trusted he would carry my burdens that I couldn't bear.

I settled for trying to accept my mom the way she was instead of focusing all of my attention on changing her. I felt like my time with her in my life was limited, so I should try to love her without always putting pressure on her to make changes. It took so much energy just to love my mom while alcohol remained the most important to her. Alcohol took away so much of what I needed from my mom to give me, and there was always the looming threat that it would take her out of my life completely.

I continued to try to do things with her, talk with her on the phone, and write to her. She saved this letter I wrote to her.

Mom,

It was so nice to see you and Al last night. We had such a good visit.

I apologize for cutting your hair so short in front. Remind me never to cut it that way again! I feel really bad about it.

I hope that when Nate and I get into a house closer to you, we can have supper together and see more of each other. That would be nice.

Good luck on your job hunting. I always pray you'll get a job soon.

Be sure and call me when you can come up to watch the wedding video. Hope to see you soon!

I love you lots, JoAnn

I don't remember if she ever saw our wedding video. I don't remember if she ever visited us in our apartment. I don't think so. There's so much my mom and I missed out on because alcohol was more important than me. What a horrible disease. I think if it can take over someone as strong, beautiful, loving, and wonderful as my mom, it can take over anyone who is susceptible to it. Some people cannot and should not drink alcohol. I am one of them.

At that time, though, I was still going out to the bar, listening to some amazing bands, drinking and having fun. Not often during the week while I had to go to work but most weekend nights. I was young, and even though I had researched that I had a 60 percent chance of becoming an alcoholic because my mom was, I thought I would be okay.

"Let the wise hear and increase in learning, and the one who understands obtain guidance" (Proverbs 1:5).

65

My second favorite Bible verse is 2 Peter 3:8–9 about God's will and God's timing versus what I want to control at the time I want. As I've written about previously, I still struggle with this. I'm not able to have enough faith to fully trust God. I always cling to more than I should because I still want to feel like I have control, even though I really don't. I look to God for the things I need. God gave us Jesus and provides everything we need, not everything we want.

I wanted my mom to stop drinking. I wanted the stress and fear I felt to go away. I didn't want to feel like I was responsible for my mom. I wanted my mom to be my mom and be there for me. I understood God gives us all free will. I understood Jesus is there for us no matter what choices we make. I understood Jesus died on a cross, was buried, and rose again so that our sins will be forgiven if we believe and accept Jesus Christ as our Savior.

But what is desired from us? At that time, I wasn't far enough along in my journey of faith to understand God desires us to do his will. He doesn't desire for us to live our lives wanting but rather giving. We can't see God, Jesus, or the Holy Spirit: "one God in three persons." So how would people know if you or I don't share the good news with anyone? Back then, I was uncomfortable to talk about

God, Jesus, and for sure the Holy Spirit with anyone that I wasn't sure already knew.

God wants us to reach as many people as we can so they, too, can know and be saved. And God is patient. I try to be patient, but really, I'm not. There were times when I thought I just wanted this to be over. The emotional pain, stress, and fear I would keep for myself instead of trusting God more was overwhelming at times. I was selfish and just wanted to get to the end of however long it would take to lose my mom to alcoholism. Wow! That's the hard truth about how I felt at times. Thank God I was able to let go and give my burdens to Jesus as much as I did. That meant giving up the control I wanted. I was very focused on me and what I wanted and needed.

I wonder how different it would have been at that time to have learned what I've learned since. Giving is receiving. I'm comfortable telling people about God, Jesus, and the Holy Spirit. I feel the Holy Spirit move in me. I try to listen to God's guidance and do his will. While none of us will ever be perfect in doing that, I continue to try to do better overall. There are times I try really hard, and other times, I'm still a slacker.

I learned what repentance is: to turn away from sin and turn toward what God says is best. It requires reading the Bible, which is God's Word. It requires restructuring how I think, what I do, and how I live my life. Not easy, and I'm still not very good at it. Notice "turning toward" what God says is best. God knows we're not perfect because he made us that way. I have found that when I love and serve others more than focusing on myself, I feel so much more fulfilled. And when I trust God more, listen and follow his guidance, and give up more control, my life goes much better. God is so good. Jesus was there for me and is there for you and me now and always.

> But do not overlook this one fact, beloved, that with the Lord one day is as a thousand years, and a thousand years as one day. The Lord is not slow to fulfill his promise as some count slowness, but is patient toward you, not wishing that any should perish, but that all should reach repentance. (2 Peter 3:8–9)

66

I've been thinking so much about faith. What is faith? The Bible says in Hebrews 11:1, "Now faith is the assurance of things hoped for, the conviction of things not seen." We all hope for things, sometimes for ourselves and sometimes for others. But what assurance do we have that what we hope for will become reality? And is hope enough? Or is action required? Is what we hope for right for us? Is what we hope for others right for them? If I have faith, then will everything I hope for come? Why do I trust God when some others don't? Can I have faith without trust?

I feel like my faith in God is unshakable. But how did it become that way and why have I felt that way for so long? Why doesn't everybody feel the same way? God is our Father and loves each and every one of us. We are his children. He gave us Jesus, our Savior and friend. Would we trust a stranger we just met? I've never seen God or Jesus, only someone's interpretation of them in art or on screen. Are there people or organizations you trust that you've only seen on video or in photos?

Perhaps the best way to know if you can trust someone is to get to know them. How do we get to know someone if we can't see them? For me, it's the people who have invested time and energy into helping me know Jesus. It's the time and energy I've put in to reading the

Bible. Different people wrote different books of the Bible at different times long before there were any modern communication methods, and yet there's consistency.

I feel blessed I somehow learned how to open my heart and mind enough to feel the presence of Jesus at a young age. It wasn't a pleasant way to learn it but certainly is a blessing. It happened when I was in the thick of getting verbal abuse from my mom while she was drunk. I cried out to him because I was in such a dark place that even the love and support I was getting from my dad and friends wasn't enough. Jesus is enough. And I felt the presence of Jesus so undeniably one time that nobody will convince me he isn't there, but I'll save that for later in my story.

Our beliefs are formed by what we let into our minds and hearts. We read, watch TV, scroll though social media, listen to others. If we let in useless, toxic, negative, untrue things, then our beliefs are going to align with that. If we let in God's Word, positive, nurturing, true things, then our beliefs are going to align with that. It always seems easier to let in the things not good for us, and somehow the things that are good for us take more work.

The devil is a master of deception and distraction. He tempted Jesus! He's constantly at work to lure us away from God and prevent or destroy our faith in God. There are millions of things to believe in and focus on that distract us from growing our faith, no matter how big or small our faith may be. First John 3:8 says, "Whoever makes a practice of sinning is of the devil, for the devil has been sinning from the beginning. The reason the Son of God appeared was to destroy the works of the devil."

Jesus was and is there for me, and he's there for you too. Know, trust, believe, have faith.

> How then will they call on him in whom they have not believed? And how are they to believe in him of whom they have never heard? And how are they to hear without someone preaching? And how are they to preach unless they are sent? As it is written, "How beautiful are the feet of those who preach the good news!" But they have not all obeyed the gospel. For Isaiah says, "Lord, who has believed what he has heard from us?" So faith comes from hearing, and hearing through the word of Christ." (Romans 10:14–17)

67

I struggled with confidence in myself and for my future. With the verbal abuse from my mom while she was drunk through my teen years, my confidence could have been crushed completely. I was told by my own mom that I was bad, made her feel bad, and it was my fault she drank and our family was falling apart. I hid all of that from most people, so I received positive feedback from other people. I had learned Jesus loves me just as I am, imperfectly perfect, created in his image. Genesis 1:27 tells us "So God created man in his own image, in the image of God he created him; male and female he created them."

The confidence I had was mostly from Jesus and me believing he would guide me, give me strength and wisdom, and hold me when I needed him to. It was still a struggle because I inherently believed what my own mother said, and it was always difficult to separate my mom from her alcoholism. But to keep living my life, I needed confidence to keep growing and reach my goals.

When I got my first job in 1984, I was left no choice but to take a data entry job just to "get my foot in the door." I had the education to be a computer programmer but didn't have any experience. Within a few months, I applied internally for a quality assurance position and was promoted. I really wanted to seek a programmer position, but that would be a fairly big jump and require moving to another department. I didn't know if I was confident enough to try to sell myself for a big jump. Without experience, I had a slim chance of getting a programmer position. I had talked to a number of people to get advice.

One person suggested I schedule a meeting with the vice president of the department that had the programmer positions. They said maybe if I introduced myself and came across very confident that I could do the job he would consider hiring me. I thought to myself, *There is no way I'm confident enough to do something like that.* But I really wanted it. I knew if I let too much time pass by that my education would quickly become out-of-date.

I prayed about it. Jesus was there for me, and over time, I felt the strength and confidence to schedule the meeting with the vice president of that department. I had to explain why I was asking for his time or he would very well choose not to meet with some random person. Just like how I'm writing this book, fully trusting that my words will flow from God working through me and not from myself, I scheduled the meeting with the explanation of why I wanted to meet with him. And he accepted my meeting invitation!

I was a nervous wreck, but I prayed and prayed about it. I asked God to work through me and for his will to be done. I was starting to learn how important that prayer is. I was working on letting go of control and trusting him. I was a year into my employment when I went to the meeting. It went really well, and by the end, the vice president said he would contact a hiring manager and that I should apply for a programmer position under that manager. And I got the job! We don't always get what we pray for, but I believe it was God's will for me. It launched a successful career in IT that I'm now thirty-seven years in.

I think, more importantly, God wanted to teach me in a big way that trusting him is best. Some call it gut instinct when they get a feeling about what they should do, and some like to believe it's what "the universe" is telling them. I believe, without doubt, it is God's guidance and Jesus by my side.

"The way of a fool is right in his own eyes, but a wise man listens to advice" (Proverbs 12:15).

68

The year following our wedding was another year of big changes. Nate and I wanted to move back "home." We realized neither one of us was cut out for living in a city and really didn't like being in an apartment. Having both grown up on farms out in the country, we really wanted to get back to that. The only downside would be our much longer commutes to work. So we started our search for our first house to buy.

Mortgage rates were around 10 percent at that time, but it didn't seem ridiculously high back then, given the rates had been even higher in the early 1980s. We learned we'd need to come up with a 20 percent down payment too. Our parents had taught us the importance of saving a portion of our pay, and that's something we've always done. I guess then we hadn't yet learned the importance and joy that comes from giving a portion as well.

We were excited to become homeowners and really excited to get back to the area we called home, close to our family and friends. We enjoyed hosting large parties at our house and took pride in making some improvements in and around our home. We enjoyed getting to know our new neighbors and felt the commutes to our jobs was doable.

The same year, I made a job change and went to work at a well-known company in Bayport, Minnesota, as a programmer. Many people in my family on my mom's side worked there (some still do), and given it was a family-owned company, I had a better chance of being hired because I had family members working there. A year later, Nate got a job there too. Both of us are grateful to the company with their generous profit-sharing payments and for being instrumental in us gaining a solid financial start in life.

I would write and tell my mom about the good things I was blessed with in my life. She would be happy for me but at the same time jealous. I'm not really sure if *jealous* is the right word, but I can only imagine how she felt because she was struggling to have a job to pay her bills. It felt awkward to tell her the good things happening for me. I would imagine she felt trapped by her need for alcohol getting in the way of having the life she had before alcohol took control. I don't remember her coming to our house. If I wanted to see her, I had to go to her apartment. And it was really hard to see her as alcohol was starting to take a physical toll on her, even though she was still in her forties.

Jesus was there for me and for all of us. Even though I was busy and making good things happen in my life, I continued to spend a lot of energy worried about my mom and trying to figure out how to help her see she needed help so she would choose to get help to stop drinking. It was this sort of black cloud or weight that was always with me, robbing me of the ability to feel like I could fully enjoy anything. It's such a sad thing that alcoholics become unable to realize the impact their alcoholism has on their loved ones. Or maybe they do, but the alcohol is still more important, so perhaps it makes them feel even worse than they already do.

We cannot imagine what someone goes through until we have gone through a similar experience. But Jesus knows. He went through emotional and physical pain as a human. He's there to help us as we go through pain and struggles here. And he's prepared a place for us in a perfect heavenly home when our time on this earth ends.

"And they said, 'Believe in the Lord Jesus, and you will be saved, you and your household'" (Acts 16:31).

69

God led me to some really special people I met at my new place of employment. He has always put the right people in my life exactly when I need them. I pray he's doing the same with me and that I've been the right person at the right time for others. Galatians 6:2 says, "Carry each other's burdens, and in this way you will fulfill the law of Christ." My experience has been that the people who have had more struggles in life are the ones who are more willing to support others having struggles.

At this point, I was an open book about my mom's alcoholism because I was so desperate for answers about what I might be able to do to help her. This was much different than all the years I had tried to hide it and try to live my life in a way that most people wouldn't guess how troubled I really was. I met a man I'll call Tom who was a recovering alcoholic. He was willing to share his experience and insights. He shared about how he hit his bottom and decided he wanted to get the help he needed to stop drinking. I admired him for being able to do that and appreciated getting his perspective. I wondered what my mom's bottom would be.

I met some women who became really good friends. Some of them would talk with me about their faith in God and how Jesus was there for them. All of them were supportive, and we had so many great conversations about all kinds of things. Most were a little older than me, so I learned a lot from them too. Everyone I worked with was awesome. We had a lot of fun and worked hard.

This was a phase of my life where my own drinking was causing problems. I've never been a daily drinker, but when I drank, I drank too much. I didn't have the ability to know when to stop for the night. I'd get nasty and argue with Nate. I was so stressed out from my mom drinking herself to death. The feeling of being drunk freed me from feeling the stress that was weighing so heavy on me. I'd get hungover and feel awful the next day. But I kept doing what I was doing. I loved having fun on the weekends and felt I deserved it.

My mom kept doing what she did too. I couldn't imagine how horrible she must have felt, and I worried that I'd get a call that she had died. I'd try to say and do nice things for her, hoping she'd find some inspiration to love herself and us enough to quit drinking. I'd try all the ways I could think of to help her see she needed help, an endless cycle of feeling like I was trying to push a huge boulder up a mountain. I felt like I was working so hard on something that was impossible.

Jesus was there for me. But I wasn't as close to him as I had been. I was starting to be a little more distant as I made myself busy with so many things. I wasn't going to church, wasn't reading my Bible, and I was praying less. I was cruising along, thinking I had my act together without really questioning all the choices I was making or the impact it was having on others. I think this is something that's easy for all of us to do.

The last photo I have of just my mom and I together was taken at this time, summer of 1987. I loved her, and she loved me. We both had our struggles in life and were doing the best we could. We both had strong faith but had strayed away a bit. Jesus was always there for us.

"And let us consider how we may spur one another on toward love and good deeds, not giving up meeting together, as some are in the habit of doing, but encouraging one another—and all the more as you see the Day approaching" (Hebrews 10:24–25 NIV).

70

Neither my brother nor I can remember what happened, so I guess maybe we never knew, but in early 1988, my mom was put on a seventy-two-hour hold by law enforcement. I had so many emotions about this. The hold was something I had put a lot of time and energy into finding out if it was something I could get done. I had a hard time believing seventy-two hours was long enough for her to get her mind clear enough to make good decisions. And I felt bad for my mom and anyone else who would have been involved in a situation that resulted in her being put on the hold. And what would happen from there?

I prayed and prayed. I called my godmother, her sister, as I always did when significant things happened in my mom's life. In my mind and in my heart, I felt this was our last chance to try to help my mom realize she needed help to stop drinking. I got my hopes up. I prayed for God to work through her and help her make decisions to try to free herself from alcoholism. It was eye-opening to me as well, prompting me to do some self-assessment. Jesus was there for me. Jesus was there for her.

Although we had both strayed away a bit, his love never fails. He never abandons us, even when we create distance. He longs for a relationship with each and every one of us. And he will guide us on the right path if we let him. The Bible says in Isaiah 41:13, "For I, the LORD your God, hold your right hand; it is I who say to you, 'Fear not, I am the one who helps you.'"

During the hold, professionals completed assessments and recommendations for my mom. But she would need to make the decision to admit herself to some form of treatment. As I usually did, I wrote my overwhelming thoughts in a letter to her. And she saved it. Below is part 1 of 2.

Mom,

All day my thoughts have been with you. I realize this is a very big decision—one that will change the rest of your life. I talked with a friend at work on Tuesday morning about me deciding to not drink any more alcohol. He said he hadn't drank alcohol for five years now and thought I was making a good decision. Today I asked him what the biggest benefit of his quitting was and he said 90% of his problems went away with the alcohol. He said the alcohol kept him away from dealing with his life, and it was scary at first but he really enjoys life now and would never go back to drinking.

He drank for twenty years and decided it wasn't worth it anymore. He committed himself for six weeks at a group therapy place. He asked me to tell you from him that it's a hard decision to make, but it's the best decision he ever made and he doesn't regret it one bit, and feels confident you would feel the same. He doesn't even know you, but he cares about you too.

Another friend of mine at work and I talk about God and prayer a lot. I asked her to pray for you too, for God to give you the will and strength to make a commitment to recover from your "prison of alcoholism." She's thinking about you too and truly cares. I need to share my concerns with people who care. I hope you don't mind. I saw my cousin today too. She always asks how you're doing. I told her you are staying at your sister's house and you're considering treatment. She was really excited. She cares so much too.

71

Part 2 of 2 of my letter to my mom:

You know, I was thinking. Your care lead is asking you to make a commitment to come to the hospital for four weeks. Maybe this is an amount of time they've found works well so each person can reach a point where they feel rewarded for the time they've put in to make a change in their life that they're happy with and proud of. It gives them time to get their thoughts straight and feel confident, not guilty or ashamed.

By "committing yourself" for four weeks, aren't you really making a commitment to yourself? You will only receive support from others, you're the ONLY one who can actually help yourself. If you do make a commitment to go to the hospital for four weeks, you have to do it for you. It's a commitment to yourself and NOBODY can make you keep going if you don't want to. You have to go because you want to go, or there is no sense in going at all because nobody will benefit from it. Nobody can make you do anything even if you do sign a paper. You have to want to get treatment and break out of the prison of alcoholism to start a new wonderful life.

Mom, I'm getting so excited for both of us. I decided I wanted to quit drinking the morning you first went to the hospital. So if you do decide to get started, I'm ready and waiting. I will switch to early shift so I can go to my class on Monday night, go to treatment with you on Tuesday and Thursday nights, go to a 4:30 class of aerobics on Wednesday and Friday nights. It would be great for me to keep busy, especially since Nate will be gone on Mondays, Tuesdays and Thursdays.

I've always wanted to go to counseling myself, but I guess I never really had the courage. Now we have an opportunity to go together two nights a week. We can really spend time together and build a good relationship to continue when treatment is done. Who knows, we might want to continue some kind of counseling together!

I really hope and pray you'll find the will and strength to make a commitment for four weeks and soon. Remember it's to yourself and for yourself. I can benefit from it too. I am willing 100%. I love you so much. Please don't let me or you down.

Your daughter, JoAnn

Wow, typing what I had handwritten back then brought a rush of adrenaline. It scares me a little how easily I'm triggered by emotions to a physical reaction still to this day, more than thirty years later. I am literally shaken right now with tears rolling down my cheeks. I'm brought back to just how badly and desperately I wanted her to make the decision to save her life. And how I truly had zero control over her decision. It would be like watching a loved one standing on top of a bridge railing, contemplating ending their life by jumping off. Only time is not minutes, it's years.

At the time, I don't think I completely understood the reasons for the recommendation for her to get treatment in the hospital. Their assessment results probably showed she was so physically addicted and damaged that it would require medication and observation to safely get her off of her alcohol addiction. Her alcoholism was already so far progressed that without that level of care, there would be a slim chance that outpatient treatment alone would be successful. I was hoping she would seek treatment of any kind. At the same time, I somehow just knew this was very likely our last chance she could realize how much damage her alcoholism was causing. Jesus was there for me.

"So we do not lose heart. Though our outer self is wasting away, our inner self is being renewed day by day. For this light momentary affliction is preparing for us an eternal weight of glory beyond all comparison" (2 Corinthians 4:16–17).

72

Encouragement, love, and prayers were not enough. My hope was crushed again. My mom did not want to get any kind of treatment. She made all kinds of excuses and did a great job spreading the blame. It's really extraordinary how skilled an alcoholic becomes at deflection.

I cannot even describe the emotions I felt. I wrote another letter, and she saved it.

> I have prayed for ten years that God would give you the will and strength to quit drinking. You must be resisting Him too.
>
> Do you realize you have been an alcoholic for the majority of both of your children's lives? My brother doesn't even remember you before you started drinking because he was too young. Why don't you quit so the majority of years of our lives are having you sober before you die an alcoholic?
>
> If you don't want to let people help you, then just forget you have a daughter. Why do you think I don't come to see you anymore? I don't want to see my mother in the process of killing herself.

You think the meetings are depressing. You have the same problem as the others do, only they're trying to face it. It's depressing to be an alcoholic—alcohol is a depressant! You're going to depress yourself right to death if you don't get help. You can't quit on your own—nobody can! Why won't you even try? Doesn't anything mean anything to you other than your booze?

Don't you understand everybody is getting real tired of trying to take care of you? Why can't you quit drinking forever and be a normal, healthy, happy person? You need counseling because you are an alcoholic. I need counseling because I am the daughter of an alcoholic and have a 60% chance of becoming an alcoholic.

Until you go through a treatment program, I give up on you. I'll be more than willing to go through a program with you if you will try because I love you.

The letter ended without signing it, and I had cut the original last two paragraphs and taped them to the top. My level of stress was so high that I was physically ill. I knew I should give what I couldn't handle to God, but I couldn't let it go. Jesus was there for me. I knew he was by my side and would carry me when I needed him to, but I couldn't let it go.

How does a person live life when being forced to hopelessly wait and watch someone you love kill themselves with one drink at a time and one day at time? The weight of helplessness and worry was feeling unbearable. How did we get here and why? How could someone so good, so strong, and with such strong faith in God be completely held prisoner by alcohol? Why isn't love enough? Why would she keep pushing herself toward a horrible way to die? I guess she didn't believe it would happen to her, despite doctors, therapists, and her family telling her what could happen if she didn't quit drinking.

So there I was, left with trying to live life while my mom drank herself to death.

> For everything there is a season, and a time
> for every matter under heaven:
> a time to be born, and a time to die;
> a time to plant, and a time to pluck up what is planted;
> a time to kill, and a time to heal;
> a time to break down, and a time to build up;
> a time to weep, and a time to laugh;
> a time to mourn, and a time to dance;
> a time to cast away stones, and a time to gather stones together;
> a time to embrace, and a time to refrain from embracing;
> a time to seek, and a time to lose;
> a time to keep, and a time to cast away;
> a time to tear, and a time to sew;
> a time to keep silence, and a time to speak;
> a time to love, and a time to hate;
> a time for war, and a time for peace.

—Ecclesiastes 3:1–8

73

I really struggled in that phase of my life. I was twenty-three years old and felt such a heavy burden feeling like a failure because as much as I wanted it and as hard as I worked for it, my mom refused to try to recover from her alcoholism. I was scared. I already knew I would want to be there for her when and if she either finally quit drinking or she went into the end stages of death from alcoholism.

It felt almost like torture to go visit her. I'd leave her heartbroken and crying. How can a thing have so much control over someone? Alcohol is a thing. There wasn't some person forcing her to drink it. Somehow, along the way, she lost control of her decisions, and the alcohol took control. I'm sure she didn't believe it could happen, but it did. And the control it had over her was more powerful than anything else in her life. God gives us free will. Alcohol does not. When someone is at risk of alcohol taking control, God-given free will needs to choose to overcome the power of alcohol. And with God's help and the many great resources we have, the want for alcohol can be removed or at least controlled.

One day at work, like any other day at work, I walked down a row of cubicles to talk with my friend. We had a short conversation, then I was returning to my desk. I don't remember what happened, but the next thing I knew, I was sitting on a chair with my friend and several other people looking at me with fear on their faces. I felt so weak and not well at all. My friend said, "We need to get you to the company nurse to get checked out." I was dazed, confused, and incredibly weak as I was brought to the nurse.

My blood pressure was dangerously low. My friend explained to the nurse that as I started walking away, I leaned against the wall of the cubicle with my feet moving as though I was walking, but I wasn't going anywhere. My friend got up to see what I was doing, and she looked at my face while my feet were still moving in place, and my eyes were open but staring straight ahead. I "wasn't there" and had no idea she was talking to me. I started going limp, and she helped me land in a chair as I was falling. She said I turned completely white as she was yelling for some help.

My blood pressure started coming back up, so the nurse determined she would not need to call an ambulance. She had me sit there and monitored me until she felt I was stable enough to get to the doctor. I was taken to my primary care doctor. He evaluated me and asked me all kinds of questions. He ordered lots of tests, including for epilepsy. He told me I had suffered a seizure. He kept me there until all of the test results came back and told me nothing was found to be abnormal or to have caused me to have a seizure.

Then he asked me, "Are you under a lot of stress?." *Um, yeah, my mom is killing herself with alcohol, and I can't help her do anything about it.* He looked at me very seriously and said, "JoAnn, this is your body telling you that your stress is starting to kill you. You're going to need to get your stress under control or you may be facing some life-threatening health conditions yourself."

I thought to myself, *How can that even be?* I felt terrified! He talked with me for a long time. He suggested I separate myself from my mom, start going to Al-Anon, and do anything else I thought would help me get my stress under control. He "gave me permission" to start taking care of myself instead of my mom. God had put another special person in my life at the right time. And Jesus was there for me.

"For nothing will be impossible with God" (Luke 1:37).

74

I went home from the clinic feeling stunned and scared. It was looking like alcoholism was likely going to take my mom's life, but I wasn't going to let it take mine! I took the advice from my doctor very seriously. He suggested I didn't drive for some period of time—that I can't remember—in case I would have another seizure. If I did, then my license would need to be suspended, but I didn't have any more seizures.

I stopped drinking completely. I found a local Al-Anon group and started going to meetings regularly. I continued to educate myself about alcoholism and especially how to live life while loving someone who is an alcoholic. And then the hard part, how do I tell my mom I can't see her anymore?

I decided to tell her in person. I would need to go to her apartment in the morning for the best chance of having her somewhat sober. I couldn't help but wonder if this would be the last time I would ever see her.

I went to her apartment. Like most times, there was the beer on the table next to her chair. Sometimes it was warm and from the night before and sometimes it was cold to get the day started. I told her about the whole day when I had the seizure. And I told her what my doctor had told me. I said, "Mom, if you would go to treatment, I will be there for you every step of the way. I'd be so happy to be there for you if you would go to treatment. But until then, I'm so sorry, but I cannot see you, Mom. I can no longer watch you kill yourself one drink at a time."

She looked at me with this almost stone emotionless face and said, "Okay."

I told her, "I love you, Mom, I always will."

She said "I love you too."

And I left. I sobbed all the way home. Tears are flowing again as I write this. Looking back, I guess each of us accepted the things we couldn't control that day.

Jesus was there for me. And he was there for her. I had to let go and let God. I'll never know how she felt or what she thought. I diligently attended Al-Anon meetings, tried to focus on healing myself, went to some counseling, got back into group exercise, read my Bible, refrained from drinking alcohol, and prayed for my mom.

I didn't know it then, but now that I have things she had written, I know this was about the time she switched from drinking beer to brandy. Did she do this because of what I did? I think so. But I had to do what I had to do, and I know I can't feel guilty about it now that I know.

This is the thing about alcoholism, though. The alcoholic is like the rock you throw into a pond. The ripples of water spread all around. Alcoholism is recognized as a family illness which includes friends as well. For family and friends of the alcoholic, Al-Anon has the "three Cs."

- We didn't *cause* it—it is not our fault that the other person drinks; it is their private battle.

- We can't *control* it—we have no power over the other person's desire to drink.
- We can't *cure* it—it is an illness that cannot be cured through any known medical remedies.

The truth is, it sucks. Accepting all of that is hard. Staying away from my mom was hard.

Without my faith in God and Jesus by my side, I don't think I could have lived a productive life. I had support from Nate, family, and friends. Al-Anon was so helpful, and the people there really helped me realize I wasn't alone in my struggles. It's so sad how many people fall into the grip of alcoholism and the wrath it causes for them and those who love them. I'm sure none of them thought it would happen to them.

"And Jesus answered them, 'Have faith in God'" (Mark 11:22).

75

My mom saved a card and letter I wrote to her a couple of months after I told her I couldn't see her anymore. I feel blessed she saved some of my letters and cards. I can't help but wonder how she chose which ones to save.

In the card, I wrote the Serenity Prayer and the following:

> I cannot change the fact that you choose to be a drinking alcoholic. You are the only one who can change that, so I have to accept it. I can change things I need to about myself, for myself.
>
> Always remember and know that I love you and always will. I care about you very much and think of you often. Please take care of yourself. I pray for you, may God bless you.

And in the letter, I wrote:

> Mom,
>
> Hi, I wanted to write and let you know how I am. I have been feeling much happier lately.

I'm learning a lot about myself. I saw a counselor twice and am going to both Al-Anon and Adult Children of Alcoholics meetings. Tonight was my fifth meeting for both. I plan to continue to go. They have helped me so much. I've learned how to give the burden and responsibility I always felt for your alcoholism to God. I pray he will give you the strength and will to commit yourself to treatment, and that you will accept that strength and will.

I'm learning how not to try to control other people and events, to accept things for what they are. I read a book entitled "Adult Children of Alcoholics" and learned so much about myself. How growing up with your alcoholism affected my personality and thoughts. With this better understanding of myself, I can work on improving.

I'm learning how to be more independent and self-confident. All of this is making my life, marriage, job and outlook better. I haven't drank any alcohol for eight weeks now and I don't intend to again. This has helped me to be happier also.

Most importantly, my relationship with God has improved. I had started to stray from him, but I'm growing closer again. It amazes me how much strength I can gain from him if I'm willing to accept it.

I love you very much, Mom, and care about you deeply. Thank you for the good upbringing you gave me as a young child. It gave me a good basis. We are both adults and both entitled to our own decisions. You are entitled to remain an alcoholic still drinking if you like and I am entitled to decide that seeing you slowly kill yourself with alcohol hurts too much.

Thank you for accepting my decision, and I want you to know I accept yours. We both have to live with the consequences of our decisions. I want you to know if you do commit yourself for treatment, I'll be there with you if you like. But until then, I just can't see you. If you die from alcoholism, I pray we'll be reunited in heaven.

Love, JoAnn

Looking back now, I see how God works through people in incredible ways. He put so many people in my life right when I needed them. Jesus was there for me. In just two months, I went from complete brokenness to making progress on my journey of healing. I think it's evident in the letter I wrote. Without God doing his work through the people he put in my life and Jesus by my side or carrying me, I wouldn't have the life I enjoy today. I pray for God to work through me to help others. He's clearly working through me to write this book. The words and the flow of the pages come almost effortlessly for me. I know I couldn't write this without him, and I believe he can through me.

"But by the grace of God I am what I am, and his grace toward me was not in vain. On the contrary, I worked harder than any of them, though it was not I, but the grace of God that is with me" (1 Corinthians 15:10).

76

I find it interesting that the "twelve steps" for Al-Anon and AA are the same. It's all about recovery, perhaps from slightly different angles. The foundation the steps are built on is believing a power greater than ourselves will help us—God as we understand him. It's an admission that we're powerless over alcohol.

I guess I didn't realize until now that my biggest fear in life is the power that alcohol can have. For many, it seems that death is their biggest fear. The pandemic that began in 2020 is proof of just how much people are willing to do and sacrifice in an effort to try to avoid death. I am not afraid of death. I'm also not in a hurry to die, and I believe there's a lot of work here that God would like me to do.

I do not understand how alcohol can be so powerful that it ruins tens of millions of lives on an ongoing basis. It overcomes one person at a time and ripples out to their family members and friends. When it gets a grip on someone, it's literally a fight for life to get back out. Not only for the alcoholic but often for those who love them.

Codependency is defined many different ways. From the research I've done, it hasn't been designated a personality or mental disorder, but it is very real and damaging to everyone who is codependent. Creating boundaries and breaking free from codependency is hard to do, just as breaking free from alcoholism is. Both require a belief in a higher power to recover. I don't think it's possible to recover from either and "be done." It's an ongoing active recovery.

Jesus was there for me. He's always there for me and for you. We need to continually grow our relationship with him, pray for wisdom of his will for us, and look to him for strength to do his will. This can be hard because it requires humility and letting go of control. Active recovery requires strength and hope. Jesus is our strength, hope, and source of joy. His love never fails. Jesus's words in the Bible are blessed assurance.

> I am the true vine, and my Father is the vinedresser. Every branch in me that does not bear fruit he takes away, and every branch that does bear fruit he prunes, that it may bear more fruit. Already you are clean because of the word that I have spoken to you. Abide in me, and I in you. As the branch cannot bear fruit by itself, unless it abides in the vine, neither can you, unless you abide in me. I am the vine; you are the branches. Whoever abides in me and I in him, he it is that bears much fruit, for apart from me you can do nothing. If anyone does not abide in me he is thrown away like a branch and withers; and the branches are gathered, thrown into the fire, and burned. If you abide in me, and my words abide in you, ask whatever you wish, and it will be done for you. By this my Father is glorified, that you bear much fruit and so prove to be my

disciples. As the Father has loved me, so have I loved you. Abide in my love. If you keep my commandments, you will abide in my love, just as I have kept my Father's commandments and abide in his love. These things I have spoken to you, that my joy may be in you, and that your joy may be full. (John 15:1–11)

77

In Al-Anon meetings, we prayed the Serenity Prayer together. It's such a simple prayer and yet so powerful to help with the journey of recovery. For the first time, I was with a group of people who truly and completely understood what I was struggling with. I hadn't realized I was dealing with anxiety from all the years of abuse, chaos, grief, and constant crises. I was in new territory, learning how to live my life without it revolving around my mom's alcoholism. I was learning how to "live and let live." It felt like a selfish thing to do, but I had to learn how to begin changing my attitude toward my situation. Fear of having another seizure was a driving motivation to stay on the journey of my own recovery.

Let go and let God. This was key to my journey of recovery. I had been trying to control something that my mom herself couldn't control. I learned that alcohol abuse results in changes in the brain, involving learning, stress, decision-making, pleasure, and self-control. I needed to try to release the burden I had been carrying and give it to God for him to handle. And I needed to give away my need to try to control the outcome. While this all felt very difficult to do and felt like I was shirking my responsibilities, my relationship with God and my trust in him grew. I really didn't have control in what my mom was doing while stuck in the grip of alcoholism. But I did have control in what I was doing. I admitted that like my mom, I too was powerless toward her alcohol addiction.

Jesus was there for me. I believe my sins are forgiven because Jesus died on a cross for the forgiveness of my sins. I wasn't going to let my mom's alcoholism take my life or ruin the rest of my life. I needed to detach from her and her alcoholism and focus on my health and well-being. I believe God has work for me to do here. The work I had been doing to try to save my mom from alcoholism was hurting me and not helping her. It was time for me to learn how to recover myself and try to live a fruitful life.

I prayed for my mom. I prayed for a miracle for her. As the months went by, I wanted to go see her, but I just couldn't. I was making progress on my own recovery and the images of her from all of my visits in the past remained in my mind, and I knew I couldn't go back to the pain of seeing her continue to die one drink at a time. I felt guilty. But I needed to continue to put my trust in Jesus to be there for her. It gave me comfort to know that Al cared about her. I knew he would call me if and when something really bad happened to her. I don't know how or why Al wanted to be a part of her life, but I thank God for him being there.

Part of my recovery journey included daily readings in the *Alateen, a Day at a Time* book. It's a compilation of personal sharing from children of alcoholics from all over the world. Since most of the abuse I experienced was during my teens, it was really helpful toward healing from some of the past pains. I found once I started focusing on my own recovery, the resources were limitless, and it was up to me how much effort I wanted to put into my recovery. I continued to refrain from alcohol as well. There's a unique feeling of control I gained simply from mitigating the risk of me falling into the grip of alcohol.

God is so good and really does provide for our needs if we let him. Humbly trusting his will and timing is best. It's difficult to do, but I continue trying.

"But he said to me, 'My grace is sufficient for you, for my power is made perfect in weakness.' Therefore I will boast all the more gladly of my weaknesses, so that the power of Christ may rest upon me" (2 Corinthians 12:9).

78

Through counseling and group meetings, I started to learn the value of having perspective and gratitude. There's always something to be grateful for and there's always someone who has it worse than you. I had felt sorry for myself, which is okay at times, but we shouldn't stay in that state of mind. It's crippling. With a focus on gratitude, my attitude changed over time. I had so much to be grateful for! I was given a suggestion to start writing in a gratitude journal. God had put so many people in my life just when I needed them. Jesus was there for me. I really felt his presence, especially when I was hurting or feeling the devil trying to pull me toward evil and bad decisions.

Writing down the things I was grateful for started with the easy and obvious things. Then I had to think deeper for things to add to my list. Then I started looking for things to add. That's when new ways of thinking began. When I began to notice all the things there are to be grateful for is when my soul began to feel whole again. I had always loved being outside in nature, but now I was noticing the details and expansiveness of the beauty. Focusing on gratitude is not only healing but helps me have a more positive attitude. It helped me feel less stress and anxiety. It quieted my soul. I still practice this today.

When I see a beautiful sky, hear the river flow, and notice the fine details in nature, I know God created it all. And I believe he uses it to show us the vastness, attention to details, power, and glory we find in him. We can't see him nor physically touch him, and we need to have faith in what we cannot see. He constantly shows us in the world around us, a wonderful reminder of his presence and love. God is omnipotent (all-powerful), omniscient (all-knowing), and omnipresent (present in all places at all times). We need never be alone or feel unloved.

I began to understand just how much I needed guidance from Jesus. And I really do have a right to make personal choices, to accept the things I cannot change and change the things that I can. Every choice has a consequence, good or bad. I have a choice about how I respond to the choices that others make. I'm entitled to make decisions that are in my best interest. I cannot control others, but I can control myself. It's okay to protect myself and guard what I let enter into my mind and heart.

We need to guard our hearts, seek truth, appreciate our blessings, and look for strength and wisdom from Jesus to avoid temptations of evil. The truth is found in the Bible.

> Do not be conformed to this world, but be transformed by the renewal of your mind, that by testing you may discern what is the will of God, what is good and acceptable and perfect. (Romans 12:2)

Again Jesus spoke to them, saying, "I am the light of the world. Whoever follows me will not walk in darkness, but will have the light of life." (John 8:12)

My child, pay attention to what I say. Listen carefully to my words. Don't lose sight of them. Let them penetrate deep into your heart, for they bring life to those who find them, and healing to their whole body. Guard your heart above all else, for it determines the course of your life. Avoid all perverse talk; stay away from corrupt speech. Look straight ahead, and fix your eyes on what lies before you. Mark out a straight path for your feet; stay on the safe path. Don't get sidetracked; keep your feet from following evil. (Proverbs 4:20–27 NLT)

79

I wonder how our culture evolved into the association of alcohol with fun, at least in Wisconsin it has. Dinner, dances, concerts, sporting events, celebrations, socializing inside and outside, even movie theaters now offer alcohol. During a global pandemic when "nonessential" businesses were forced to close, liquor stores were deemed "essential" and remained open while churches were not. As a person in my early twenties, not drinking alcohol, I noticed just how much socializing and entertainment revolve around alcohol.

I found the behavior toward me choosing not to consume alcohol was interesting. With the tradition of "buying a round of drinks," I would sometimes be overlooked because I had a water or soda sitting in front of me. In a restaurant for dinner, the server will ask someone with me drinking alcohol if they want another drink but not ask me. In the early eighties, it was common for bars to offer two-for-one or three-for-one drink specials, but it only applied to alcoholic drinks. There's only one place I remember going to that offered free unlimited soda to anyone who was designated sober cab.

No offense to anyone who owns or works in the businesses where alcohol is sold or served. It's just really clear to me how prevalent alcohol is in our culture. It's encouraging to see more businesses offering fun and tasty mocktails now. As someone who has enjoyed a lot of entertainment and socializing while sober for the better part of my life, it gets really old to only have the options of water, juice, or soda. I really like the taste of some alcoholic drinks but would need to settle for not as tasty nonalcoholic options.

I think it's really difficult for recovering alcoholics to enjoy entertainment and socializing while fighting to stay sober because our culture associates alcohol with fun. So, oftentimes, a recovering alcoholic needs to make a choice to avoid doing fun things in order to avoid the temptation of drinking that's associated with it. I really admire and respect people who can find the strength to recover from alcoholism and stay sober. I'm not sure most people understand what it takes.

I'm going to leap a little ahead in time to share a story about a friend who has done this, someone who told me that I made a difference for him and helped him to stay sober at a time when he felt weak. We were all at a wedding dance for a friend. Nate and I were having lots of fun with a lot of our friends all celebrating the newly married couple. This friend had recently started his recovery from alcoholism. He knew about my mom's alcoholism and the impacts it had on me.

Suddenly, he came up to me and said, "I'm going to drink."

I looked him in the face and said, "No, you're not," and I asked him to step outside with me. I talked with him and shared a lot of detail about my mom's final stages of alcoholism and pleaded with him that it's not the way he'd want his life to end. I begged him to please not put his son through it. I talked about God and the strength he could find and the burdens he could release.

We talked about how Jesus was there for me and there for him. Our conversation ended with him staying firm in his commitment to continue his recovery, and he left in an effort to avoid the temptation there. Years later, he told me he felt that moment was the pivotal moment for him remaining in his recovery or relapsing. He thanked me. I told him I'm so proud of him and just grateful I was there. I thank God. At the time of writing this, he's been sober for more than thirty years. I pray for God to work through me, and I believe he did that night. God brings good even from our greatest pain.

"And we know that for those who love God all things work together for good, for those who are called according to his purpose" (Romans 8:28).

80

Nate and I made the decision to build a log home in the woods. He had worked with our friends who built them, so we began working on the plans for our dream home. We purchased the land from a family friend and began work to prepare the location for our new log home. We listed our current house for sale, and it sold fairly quickly. Nate's cousin and her husband were gracious enough to welcome us into their home to live for almost a year while we worked and waited for our new home to be completed. We'll always be grateful to them and appreciate the bond that grew with them.

Nate and I had welcomed my friend and her young son into our home when they needed a place to stay during a transition. Having experienced being on both sides of offering and needing a place to live during transition, we've continued to welcome family and friends to live with us when needed. We've been blessed and we try to pay it forward and bless others. Luke 6:38 tells us, "Give, and it will be given to you. Good measure, pressed down, shaken together, running over, will be put into your lap. For with the measure you use it will be measured back to you."

Our lives were moving forward while my mom's was coming to an end. God bless my brother for being there for her, loving and accepting her just as she was. I'm so grateful he was there for her. And her friend, Al, was getting her out to do things like weekend trips, visits to a park, and buying her gifts. I'll never forget how happy she was when he bought her a new winter coat.

Although I wasn't visiting my mom, I continued to write letters and get updates from my brother. It was too difficult for me to even talk on the phone with my mom because I could hear the hold that alcohol had on her, and she was getting more depressed. She kept trying to gain employment because she was broke. I'm guessing her friend Al (also her landlord) helped her live in her apartment, even though she couldn't pay full rent. It was a constant internal battle for me not to visit her, even though I wanted to so badly sometimes because I assumed it was breaking her heart.

My brother had a girlfriend, had finished school to learn to do autobody work, and was living independently and working hard. While being the only one left in my mom's immediate family in her life, he too was moving on with his own life. He had a lot to deal with, and I'm grateful our relationship continued to stay strong.

Throughout our entire lives, we've been so close, having a sister-brother bond that has never been broken. Jesus was there for me and my brother. We both have unshakable faith. We trust one another with everything and our love for one another has never failed. We've been blessed beyond all measure to have one another to go through life.

Together, I hope my mom knew we both did our best to be there for her and loved her throughout all the years we had together. I'm grateful we had a photo of the three of us taken at my wedding. I think it may be the only photo I have of the three of us. Jesus was there for us, and we shared our faith in him. We all believe he died for our sins, we are forgiven, and he's prepared a place for us in heaven.

> Let not your hearts be troubled. Believe in God; believe also in me. In my Father's house are many rooms. If it were not so, would I have told you that I go to prepare a place for you? And if I go and prepare a place for you, I will come again and will take you to myself, that where I am you may be also. And you know the way to where I am going. (John 14:1–4)

81

My mom saved the card I sent her for Mother's Day, 1989. By this point in time, my mom had been an alcoholic for more years than not in my life, and I hadn't seen her in over a year. The card I chose had a prayer on the front. It said:

> A Mother's Day Prayer for You… Dear Lord,
> Please bless all mothers for every good thing their
> strong faith in you and their love and trust bring.
> Stay close to them always and Lord, if you will—
> grant each the blessings you alone can fulfill.

She had stapled to the card the letter I wrote inside.

Mom,

> I am so happy you had a talk with God and
> asked for strength with your drinking problem,
> and also that God answered your prayers (and
> mine) that you would get a job.
> I am finding over and over again I can
> count on God for so many things. I rely on Him

a lot. It seems He always makes things happen for me that are for the best. If things don't go the way I think they ought to, I believe there is always a good reason. I would like to thank you for bringing me up in faith. I'm thankful for you teaching about God. Without Him, things could be tough.

I would like to get together with you sometime soon and have a good chat. I am going to make something for you too. I pray you'll find the strength you need with your drinking problem. I would really like to spend more time with you, but as you know, it's really hard for me when you're drinking. I like the Mom that doesn't drink—she's a really special person. But remember, whatever happens, I'll always love you very, very much! If there's anything I can do to help, please let me know. I pray for you every day.

I wrote about updates on my job and preparations for building our house. And then ended the letter with the following.

Let's try to get together soon. I miss you. Have a very happy birthday Mom! (Her birthday was shortly after Mother's Day.) I love you! Take care of yourself! One day at a time!

Love, JoAnn

Jesus was there for me. In addition to my mom having been an alcoholic for more than half of my life, Jesus had been so clearly present for me. Unless I stubbornly try to think I'm in control, which I continually need to remind myself I'm not, I don't picture myself alone. Jesus is always beside me or carrying me. I believe he was there for my mom too and that she believed in him.

I realize I refer to God and Jesus seemingly interchangeably. In the Bible, the book of John, chapter 10, Jesus explains, "I am the Good Shepherd" and "I and the Father are One."

> The Jews were picking up stones to stone him for blasphemy for saying he is the Son of God.
>
> So the Jews gathered around him and said to him, "How long will you keep us in suspense? If you are the Christ, tell us plainly."
>
> Jesus answered them, "I told you, and you do not believe. The works that I do in my Father's name bear witness about me, but you do not believe because you are not among my sheep. My sheep hear my voice, and I know them, and they follow me. I give them eternal life, and they will never perish, and no one will snatch them out of my hand. My Father, who has given them to me, is greater than all, and no one is able to snatch them out of the Father's hand. I and the Father are one." (John 10:24–30)

82

Temptation. There are so many things in our world that are temptations. The temptation to drink alcohol in a culture that includes it in almost everything we think of as fun is something that can be tough to resist. God made his Son, Jesus, human, like us, to live and experience everything humans do. And even worse because Jesus was persecuted for claiming he was the Son of God. And he knew he would die a grueling death for the forgiveness of our sins.

Two books in the Bible tell a very similar story, both in chapter 4, where the devil was tempting Jesus. This is the version from Luke 4:1–13:

> And Jesus, full of the Holy Spirit, returned from the Jordan and was led by the Spirit in the wilderness for forty days, being tempted by the devil. And he ate nothing during those days. And when they were ended, he was hungry. The devil said to him, "If you are the Son of God, command this stone to become bread." And Jesus answered him, "It is written, 'Man shall not live by bread alone.'" And the devil took him up and showed him all the kingdoms of the world in a

moment of time, and said to him, "To you I will give all this authority and their glory, for it has been delivered to me, and I give it to whom I will. If you, then, will worship me, it will all be yours." And Jesus answered him, "It is written, 'You shall worship the Lord your God, and him only shall you serve.'" And he took him to Jerusalem and set him on the pinnacle of the temple and said to him, "If you are the Son of God, throw yourself down from here, for it is written, 'He will command his angels concerning you, to guard you,' and 'On their hands they will bear you up, lest you strike your foot against a stone.'" And Jesus answered him, "It is said, 'You shall not put the Lord your God to the test.'" And when the devil had ended every temptation, he departed from him until an opportune time.

It says "until an opportune time." The devil is always working on us, and there are endless "opportune times" when we are tempted. Without Jesus and the Bible, how would we know evil from good? Do we believe what we're told by other humans who are more than happy to spew their knowledge out to us? Is their knowledge based in the Bible? Do you believe what I'm writing in this book?

I don't want this book to be about me. I want it to be about how Jesus was there for me and is there for me and you always. I'm using my life experience as just one example of one person Jesus is helping. Jesus is there for each and every one of us if we let him. I pray for

God to do his work through me. I sat down to write this entry and had no idea what to write. This is the case most days. Today, much of this entry will come directly from the Bible because I can't speak to temptation like Jesus. And I certainly can't resist temptation like Jesus did as a human.

Jesus sympathizes with our weakness. He gives us mercy, grace, and forgiveness. God made each of us in his own image, perfectly imperfect and with free will. We must depend on Jesus. Without him, we have no power over sin, the devil, and his temptations. There is no promise our lives will be easy. There is a promise that Jesus will help us and give us everything we need. He's our guide, strength, protector, Redeemer, Savior, who loves us unconditionally. His love never fails.

> For we do not have a high priest who is unable to sympathize with our weaknesses, but one who in every respect has been tempted as we are, yet without sin. Let us then with confidence draw near to the throne of grace, that we may receive mercy and find grace to help in time of need. (Hebrews 4:15–16)

83

I've realized that for two-thirds of my life, someone in my family was dying from a disease. And for half of my life, someone in my family was dying from alcoholism—my mom and sister-in-law from alcoholism; my dad from heart disease and my parents-in-law from cancer.

I wonder how many people are in a similar situation? Why, God, oh, why do I need to live the majority of my life with the overwhelming sadness of someone in my family dying? Of course, we're all dying. Every day we live, we are one day closer to death. We don't know when. It could be sudden and unexpected or it could be a disease that progresses for weeks, months, or years. Either way, it hurts.

James 1:2–4 (NIV) says, "Consider it pure joy, my brothers and sisters, whenever you face trials of many kinds, because you know that the testing of your faith produces perseverance. Let perseverance finish its work so that you may be mature and complete, not lacking anything." But how do we feel joy when we face trials? Wouldn't we feel sorrow instead?

It seems we can feel both joy and sorrow at the same time. Having been at the bedside of four of my beloved family members in their final minutes, hours, and days, I can attest there was joy and laughter amidst the sorrow and tears. Conversations about memories created laughter. Prayers and Bible readings brought assurance my loved ones were going to heaven. I felt joy that their suffering would end and they would find rest in the arms of Jesus. Sometimes there is joy and laughter during funerals and often afterward when people gather together. Nowadays, we even call it a celebration of life.

So what can stop us from feeling joy? Do we seek joy from what is in the world or do we seek it from God? Worldly joy will come and go. Worldly joy must meet our expectations. Joy that comes from God is lasting and will exceed our expectations. But how do we learn to seek this joy and experience it? Joy is a free and perfect gift just like forgiveness and salvation. We need to accept it and choose it. Sin robs us of joy. Unlike sorrow, we cannot sin and feel joy at the same time. We all sin and we all go through trials. Jesus was there for me. He's there for each and every one of us. He wants us to repent of our sins and find joy. He wants to take our burdens, comfort us in our sorrow, get through our trials, and feel joy.

Going through trials makes us stronger and should bring us closer to Jesus. Jesus went through trials, betrayals, and even a horrible death for the forgiveness of our sins and promise of eternal life. He rose from the dead. In our darkest moments, we can find joy in him. This evil world has nothing to offer that truly brings us joy. Living life in this world is a journey of learning that we need a relationship with Jesus. We go through trials and temptations, but Jesus is always there for us. When we feel awful about ourselves, when we sin, when we feel like we can't go on any longer, Jesus is there for us. A beautiful sunrise or sunset, shimmering snow, or frost on a branch, kind words from a stranger, a hug from a friend are all gifts from God and help us feel joy. Trials come. We need to seek joy by seeking Jesus.

Therefore, since we are surrounded by so great a cloud of witnesses, let us also lay aside every weight, and sin which clings so closely, and let us run with endurance the race that is set before us, looking to Jesus, the founder and perfecter of our faith, who for the joy that was set before him endured the cross, despising the shame, and is seated at the right hand of the throne of God. (Hebrews 12:1–2)

84

In the fall of 1989, I learned that I was going to be an aunt, and my mom would be a grandma. I was so excited! I send a card to my mom that she kept. I wrote "I've been thinking about you often—I love you very much!" I called her "Grandma" in the card, shared how excited I was to be an aunt, and a few updates about the progress on our new home.

I thought maybe, just maybe, this unplanned pregnancy that would make her a grandma would be significant enough to finally motivate her to get the help she needed. I tried not to get my hopes up, but for the first time in a long time, I had a glimmer of hope.

Plans were made for a wedding in just two months. My mom was able to attend her son's beautiful December wedding. It was the first time I had seen her in well over a year and the second time that my dad and her were in the same place since their divorce. She wore the same dress she had worn to my wedding. I talked with her for a while, gave her a big hug, and told her I love her so much. I apologized that it hurt me too much to visit her. I reminded her that if she would seek help for her alcoholism, I would be there for her every step of the way.

While I was happy for my brother, I felt so bad. Our family was a disconnected mess. I was becoming a stranger to my mom and alcohol is what she loved most. Neither my brother nor I were spending much time with my dad because his second wife was not pleasant toward us. My brother and I remained close, but we didn't see each other often because he lived in the same apartment building as my mom. God bless him for choosing to live so near to her and be there for her.

Jesus was there for me. He was there for all of us. And he's there for you. Our family was separated from each other but not from Jesus. We all kept faith in Jesus. We all shared our love for Jesus and love for one another. I think we all struggled to keep our faith in Jesus strong at times. So many unanswered questions and unanswered prayers.

Have you noticed how people and happenings in your life are woven together? Back then, I don't think I noticed this as much. Now I try to pay more attention. I see that God is at work in ways that are easy to completely miss. I've noticed how something bad happening to one person in my life may play a part in healing another person in my life. I've noticed how sermons/messages at church cover exactly what I need to hear on that very day. I've noticed how someone suddenly appears in my life exactly when I need them. I've noticed how when I need to learn something about someone that it happens right when I need to know it. I often open the Bible to a random page and find just what I needed to read that day.

So while life is full of unanswered questions and seemingly unanswered prayers, maybe if we pay more attention to the way God brings good to our lives, even from something bad, we'll find more answers. "God works in mysterious ways" is something that myself and others often say. It's a mystery to us but not at all to God. He is always working for our good through people willing to let him and circumstances in our lives. I don't believe that anything is truly left to chance but rather a culmination of God working through people to whom he has given free will and guiding them where they're needed at the right time.

"Call to me and I will answer you, and will tell you great and hidden things that you have not known" (Jeremiah 33:3).

85

In Luke 14:11, Jesus says, "For everyone who exalts himself will be humbled, and he who humbles himself will be exalted." The importance of being humble is covered many times in the Bible. I feel like my desire to try to control people and outcomes is proof that I struggle to be humble. I really don't know what's best for myself, let alone for anyone else. God does, and I need to trust him. I think humility requires patience. God's way, his timing. He is all-knowing, and we are not.

Jesus was and is there for me, but to truly give it all to God feels impossible. I am not humble enough. I don't have enough faith or trust. Perhaps it's because my focus is on the here and now more often than on eternity. I believe fully that because of Jesus, my sins are forgiven, and when I die, I'll have eternal life in heaven. I believe the alternative is eternal life in hell where suffering never ends. Living life on this earth with all the evil temptations and struggles will lead us to one or the other.

This earth is also filled abundantly with beautiful reminders of how great God is and how humbled we should be. In my opinion, one of the most humbling experiences is the birth of a child. I've had the privilege of giving birth and witnessing birth. God creates each one of us in his image. Only God is capable of creating a human body so complex. God created the earth and everything on it, and that is humbling. Being in awe and wonder at the beauty God created enables powerful healing from the day-to-day struggles.

In Mark 16, Jesus speaks to the disciples after he rose from the dead and before he ascended into heaven. In verses 15–16, he said to them, "Go into all the world and proclaim the gospel to the whole creation. Whoever believes and is baptized will be saved, but whoever does not believe will be condemned."

This is the expectation for us as well. My mom and others told me about Jesus, and I believe. How do I be strong enough and yet humble myself to tell others about Jesus? So often, Christians are viewed as judgmental and "holier than thou." Proclaiming the gospel—the birth, life, death, burial, and resurrection of Jesus Christ is not easy or comfortable.

Some people may never proclaim the gospel to someone. Some may be comfortable with people they know and some with people they don't know. Some people will listen, and some will not. Some people already know Jesus, and some do not. Jesus asks us to do our best to make sure everyone will know about him because he does not want anyone to be condemned to eternity in the lake of fire.

Revelation 21:8 tells us, "But as for the cowardly, the faithless, the detestable, as for murderers, the sexually immoral, sorcerers, idolaters, and all liars, their portion will be in the lake that burns with fire and sulfur, which is the second death."

Without Jesus, there is no forgiveness of our sins. Romans 6:23 says, "For the wages of sin is death, but the free gift of God is eternal life in Christ Jesus our Lord." How humbling it is to begin to understand the greatness, perfection, and power of Jesus Christ. And yet Jesus humbled himself.

> Have this mind among yourselves, which is yours in Christ Jesus, who, though he was in the form of God, did not count equality with God a thing to be grasped, but emptied himself, by taking the form of a servant, being born in the likeness of men. And being found in human form, he humbled himself by becoming obedient to the point of death, even death on a cross. Therefore God has highly exalted him and bestowed on him the name that is above every name, so that at the name of Jesus every knee should bow, in heaven and on earth and under the earth, and every tongue confess that Jesus Christ is Lord, to the glory of God the Father. (Philippians 2:5–11)

86

In March 1990, my nephew was born. I was at the hospital for most of the several days where the care team managed what had become a high-risk delivery. I wanted to be there to support my brother and his wife. Everything worked out, and we were so relieved that both Mom and baby were doing well, given all they had gone through. This was my first personal experience with the miracle of birth, and although I didn't witness the actual birth, to say I was wowed is an understatement.

My mom met her grandson after they came home from the hospital. I don't know of any photo with my mom holding her grandson, but I hope my brother has one. I have a full album of photos of my new baby nephew. The only photo I found in my mom's belongings of him was of me holding him and her looking over at us from the other end of the couch. It was taken at my brother's apartment.

Seeing this photo now makes me so sad. I wonder what she was thinking at that moment. I wonder if she thought about everything she would miss because she was in the grip of alcoholism so badly that she wouldn't live to see her grandchildren grow up. Maybe she kept her distance because she knew it hurt me to smell alcohol when she got close to me. Maybe she wondered if she'd ever see me holding my own baby. Why wouldn't the birth of her first grandchild stir up a desire within her to seek help to stop drinking? The grip of alcohol is so powerful! It robs the alcoholic and their family members of so much.

And why did the law prevent me from being able to make her stay in a treatment center for at least thirty days instead of seventy-two hours? Studies show that in the first seventy-two hours (which is the typical hold timeframe), an alcoholic may go through withdrawal symptoms like hallucinations and seizures (DTs). And as the seventy-two-hour period starts coming to an end, most are experiencing the worst and potentially fatal withdrawal symptoms. This is the point in which they are free to leave or sign themselves into a treatment program. I would think this is why most choose to leave and desperately get alcohol to stop the horrible withdrawal symptoms. The level of frustration I still feel about this is unmeasurable. I still believe that if allowed by law, my mom could have been saved from alcoholism.

On the couch that day, I held a new beautiful life in my arms while sitting close but yet so far away from my mom who was dying from alcoholism one drink at a time, and there was nothing I could do about it. She had started wearing a button that said "Uff Da." We are Scandinavian and used that exclamation all the time in our family, but I never really thought about what it meant. I have found varying definitions of "Uff Da." One says it's a mild and polite vernacular interjection used when something is unpleasant, uncomfortable, hurtful, annoying, sad, or irritating. Perhaps my mom decided to wear it daily because that's exactly how she felt all the time.

Jesus was there for me. He was there for my mom and all of us. We all felt pain, and yet there was joy. I just realized that I wrote "and yet" in the previous sentence. It came so naturally because I often think that way. In the message at church last Sunday, the pastor asked if we have the "and yet" kind of faith. Circumstances may be very difficult, and yet there is Jesus. I hadn't thought about it that way, but when asked, I can say yes, I absolutely have the "and yet" kind of faith. No matter what happens and how hard my circumstances may be, Jesus is there for me. And he's there for you—always!

"Have I not commanded you? Be strong and courageous. Do not be frightened, and do not be dismayed, for the Lord your God is with you wherever you go" (Joshua 1:9).

87

Outside of the few times I saw my mom related to my brother's wedding and baby, I continued to follow my doctor's orders to detach from my mom, attend group meetings, and work on my healing. Life was busy with our jobs and working on our new home. I so often felt bad about keeping distance from my mom, but I kept sending her cards and letters to let her know that I loved her, and I'd be there for her if she would seek help to stop drinking. I prayed and prayed. I felt like we were running out of time. By now, it had been months since she had her last job, and like the others before that, it didn't last long. I don't know how she got by from a financial perspective. All I can think of is that Al must have helped her, and I don't remember if I ever thanked him properly for that.

My dad and his second wife had decided to sell our family farm and buy a house in a nearby town. My dad had spent most of his life living on that farm, having grown up there and inheriting it from his parents. I really didn't think he'd be happy living in a house in town. He had an auction and sold all the farm equipment and everything that wouldn't fit in the house. My brother and I wished so much that one of us would have been in a position to buy the farm and keep it in the family.

As my dad was packing and sorting stuff in the outbuildings on the farm, he found booze bottles my mom had hidden. It's still so hard to believe the lies, secrets, and manipulation that alcoholics will employ to try to hide their drinking when they know their family loves them but not their drinking.

Nate and I finished up the final details of building and moved into our new home. We planned to have a big party to celebrate our housewarming and my birthday. I invited my mom. I thought that maybe if she had something to look forward to and feel included that it would help her. My brother was letting me know that he was getting quite concerned about her as she was well into the final stages of alcoholism. While I'm so grateful he was there for her, I felt so bad that he had so much going on—long hours at work, supporting his wife and baby boy, and being there for our mom. Since his apartment was right above hers, he checked on her a couple of times a day. Big things were happening in our lives while our mom's life was withering away.

Then, one day, a day when I was home, my phone rang. It was my brother, and he was in a panic. He said, "Jo, please come now. I think Mom's dying! I checked on her this morning. She's in her bed, and something is really wrong."

I told him I'd be right there. On the short trip there, so many thoughts raced through my mind. Shame on me, I had hardly seen her in what may have been the last two years of her life. I should have been able to help her. What could I have done differently? I knew this day would come, but how am I going to live with myself if this ends this way? How bad will this be for her to go through? Will she be alive when I get there?

Jesus was there for me. He was there for all of us. I knew at that moment that I would keep my promise to be there for her every step of the way if she would quit drinking. I didn't know what would happen when I got there and I knew Jesus would be with us. But I was so scared!

"It is the Lord who goes before you. He will be with you; he will not leave you or forsake you. Do not fear or be dismayed" (Deuteronomy 31:8).

88

I arrived at my mom's and ran into her apartment, straight back to her bedroom. My brother was in there, and my mom didn't acknowledge my arrival. She looked pale. I gently pushed on her shoulder while saying, "Mom, Mom." When she looked up at me, I asked her what was going on. She told me that when she had gone to the bathroom, there was a lot of blood in the toilet. I said, "I'm so sorry, we need to get you to the hospital."

She said, "No, just let me die here."

I said, "I'm sorry, I can't do that. I can't just let you lie here and die. Either I need to call an ambulance or we need to get you into my car to take you."

She continued to resist, saying she really wanted to die there.

I said, "Mom, my birthday party is coming up, and you're invited. I'd really like you to be there. I'd just really like you to still be here."

After a lot more back and forth, I think she just finally gave in because she knew I wasn't about to let her lie there and die. She said she couldn't afford an ambulance, but she would go with me. Looking back on those moments, I have some regrets because I was focusing only on what I wanted and not what might end up happening to her. But I give myself some grace too. I mean, who in that situation would give in and let your own mother lie there and die without doing anything about it? It wasn't like we were in a hospice situation. I believed she would be saved if we could just get her to a doctor.

She was incredibly weak and couldn't sit up by herself. I don't know what I was thinking at that time. I clearly should have called an ambulance. But she agreed to go if I took her, and I wasn't able to think clearly. My brother was following my lead. Together, we managed to get her onto her feet. I don't know if I remember this correctly, but I'm pretty sure she decided she should look more presentable and asked us to change her clothes or comb her hair or something. She did always care and took the time to look nice. Anyway, my brother and I managed to get her into my car. I don't remember why, but my brother stayed there, and off I went with my mom.

I drove her to the River Falls Clinic and not the hospital. I don't know if I was thinking the clinic would be adequate for her needs or cheaper because she couldn't afford anything. I got out and started to help my mom out of the car. It took every muscle and all the strength I could muster to get her on her feet, only to realize she wasn't going to be able to walk to the door of the clinic. I wasn't strong enough to carry her, so I found the strength I needed to help her sit back down on the car seat safely. I ran inside the clinic.

I talked to the person at the front desk, and they had me wait so a nurse could come out to talk with me. When I explained what had happened, she said I should take my mom directly to the hospital. I remember feeling like a crazy person. I couldn't get my head straight. I apologized to my mom and told her I needed to drive her to the hospital. By the time we arrived, the nurse must have called the hospital to let them know we were on our way. There were people waiting to get my mom out of the car and into the hospital.

Jesus was there for me, even when I couldn't think straight. I breathed a quick sigh of relief, knowing she was finally getting care and stayed there while they evaluated her and ran tests.

"Therefore do not be anxious about tomorrow, for tomorrow will be anxious for itself. Sufficient for the day is its own trouble" (Matthew 6:34).

89

When the doctor came out to talk to me, it was the same doctor I had seen when I had my seizure, the same one who gave me orders to detach from my mom, join Al-Anon, and focus on healing myself before something worse happened to me. I'll call him Dr. W.

He told me my mom was in really bad shape. She was suffering from chronic liver failure due to cirrhosis. Cirrhosis is the scarring of your liver from repeated or long-lasting injury, such as from drinking alcohol excessively over a long period of time. This was why she was so weak and tired, bleeding internally, and had fluid buildup in her abdomen. He said she was getting disoriented as well. He started her on some treatments to try to improve her current condition but told me the cirrhosis and liver failure was likely too far advanced to have a chance of recovery. He said they would keep her admitted and was very uncertain about how she would do.

I went in to talk with her, and together we tried to understand what Dr. W. had just explained to each of us. I cried. I knew this day would probably come, but I was not prepared for it to actually arrive. She was too tired and weak to react much, but I could see in her eyes that she understood that this is how she ended up. I sat with her until visiting hours ended that night. She was really tired, so we didn't talk much at all. When it was time for me to leave, I hugged her, told her I loved her and that I'd be back the next day. She told me she loved me too.

I made sure the hospital had all of my contact information as I would be their primary contact. I left and cried the whole way home. I updated my brother and my godmother (her sister) as Nate tried to console me when I got home. I had hope she would improve. I prayed and I prayed. That same night, the phone rang. It was Dr. W. My mom had gone into a hepatic coma. He told me he would do everything he could to bring her out of it, but he didn't know if she would. He was very clear about how ill she was. I told him I would pray, and he agreed that was the best thing I could do. He said I should still visit her and talk to her because he believed that although she was in the coma, she might still hear me. Again I updated my brother and godmother.

My dad was still working nights, but the next morning, I called him. I needed my daddy. He told me that he was there to support me, but he was very sorry he would not be able to be involved in any way with what was going on with my mom. His second wife had started treating me almost like I was my dad's "other woman," which was really weird. She was jealous of him spending time with me, so anything with his ex-wife wouldn't be okay. He was expected to spend time with her kids and grandkids, though. And so this journey for my mom and me began. She finally was done drinking but only because she couldn't anymore. And I'd be responsible for making decisions for my mom if she couldn't make them. That scared me!

I went to the hospital daily to talk to my mom and pray while she was in the coma, all because alcohol got a grip on her and she couldn't stop killing herself one drink at a time. I had to go to work and keep up on my responsibilities there. Nate had to cover my share of the work at home. I spent as much time as I could with her. I had promised that if she stopped drinking that I would be there for her. And Jesus was there for me and gave me all I needed.

"He who calls you is faithful; he will surely do it" (1 Thessalonians 5:24).

90

The date of our housewarming and my birthday celebration was nearing. I thought about canceling it, but Nate had worked so hard on planning everything we needed for it. We would be having a crew roast an entire hog, and we'd feed and provide drinks for all of our family and friends. And some of our family had already made travel arrangements to attend. We would need to keep our party date and hope for the best.

One morning, as I was about to leave our house, our phone rang. It was Dr. W. He said my mom was coming out of the coma. I was so happy! I wanted to be there, so I called in to work and went straight to the hospital. She was slowly becoming alert. I talked to her and held her hand. Dr. W. encouraged me to continue talking to her because it would "help her find her way back." And she did find her way back out of the coma. Dr. W. said she was still very ill and would need to stay in the hospital for probably a week or two. He recommended that from there, she should go to an inpatient treatment program. She would need continuous monitoring of her health while starting a treatment program.

Deep inside, I wondered if when I talked with her about this if she would actually finally agree to go to treatment. So many times in the past, she blatantly refused. But perhaps this scared her. But even if she recovered enough to go, was it too late? So many questions were spinning around in my head. I assumed Dr. W. talked with her about his recommendation before I did. And if he was as clear about how critical her health had become with her as he was with me, then she'd need to make the choice to try to live or to die.

When I talked with her about it, she was ready to go to treatment. She wanted to try to live and said she understood she would only get this one chance. I was so relieved! I never thought I would hear her agree to go to treatment. I thought she would die without ever trying to live and recover from her alcoholism. I told her I would be there for her every step of the way, just as I had promised.

I learned it would be my responsibility to find an "in hospital" treatment program that would have an opening in the next week or two. I was bound and determined. So while Nate and I were going to work, completing final preparations for our party, and visiting my mom, I was learning all there was to learn about how to get my mom into an "in hospital" treatment program when she didn't have any health insurance.

Jesus was there for me. He was there for us. By the grace of God, I was able to make arrangements for her to go to an inpatient treatment program at the hospital in Red Wing. I felt grateful it was within a half hour of our home. My mom showed signs of improvement in the hospital, and her mind even started to clear up from the fog of alcohol. Physically, she was a mess and very uncomfortable. But mentally, the mom I knew and loved as a young child was slowly reappearing. I thought to myself that even if her condition would worsen, I would be so grateful for every moment I would get with her.

I finally got to give more positive updates to my brother and my godmother. My godmother was keeping the rest of my mom's siblings up-to-date so I didn't need to call them all. I realized my mom's condition was fragile and could deteriorate at any moment, but for the first time in a really long time, my loving mom was breaking free from the alcohol that had held her hostage. God is so good!

"I have blotted out your transgressions like a cloud and your sins like mist; return to me, for I have redeemed you" (Isaiah 44:22).

91

My mom was holding her own in the hospital, and although it was hard to see her with her illness taking such a toll on her physically, I was starting to enjoy our conversations. We talked about the plans for her to move to the hospital in Red Wing to start her treatment program. She told me she was scared and concerned about how bad her health had become. I told her I was scared too.

She had to miss our big housewarming and my twenty-sixth birthday celebration at our new home. It was a wonderful party. And for that day, I let myself really enjoy the company of all of our friends and family who attended. We felt so blessed to be in our beautiful log home and feeling so loved and celebrated that day. My mom was safe and getting good care. And in another week, she'd be admitting herself to treatment. I felt more content than I had in a long time.

The next week went quickly as I finalized the plans for my mom to move to the Red Wing hospital. I would take her home to stay at our house for one night and then drive her to Red Wing in the morning. She wanted to see our new home. She seemed truly happy for us when we got there. It had been a long time since I felt like she was truly happy for me. The alcohol had seemed to make her kind of numb, robbing her of the ability to show happiness for me and my brother.

The big day came, the day I would drive my mom to start a treatment program for her alcoholism! I helped with all of the admitting paperwork and made sure they had my contact information. They explained that for the first part of the treatment program, I would not be allowed to visit. That was the way the program worked. I was welcome to send her mail, but engaging family in her treatment program would come later. I have to admit this hurt my feelings. I was just getting my mom back, and now I wouldn't be able to visit her. But I understood that they knew best and I would need to wait. I couldn't help but feel really nervous, though, because I understood how fragile her health was. I prayed she could get through the program and for her health to improve. Jesus was there for me, and he was there for her.

Fast-forward to when my daughters were born. When I would hold my older daughter to give her a bottle while sitting on our couch, she would stare at a specific place in the living room and smile really big. This wouldn't seem uncommon, except she did it almost every time I gave her a bottle on the couch. I wondered why. Then my younger daughter was born. And she did the same thing, the same place and just as consistently. My mom had stayed with us there that one night. I choose to believe that each of them felt a special connection to my mom while looking in that place, and she made them smile.

On one of the worksheets used in my mom's treatment, she had written "I feel frustration. I feel bad I hurt a lot of relatives and friends in my drunken state. I'm sorry I fell into the grip of alcohol." Jesus forgives us. His forgiveness surpasses all understanding.

And the grace of our Lord overflowed for
me with the faith and love that are in Christ

Jesus. The saying is trustworthy and deserving of full acceptance, that Christ Jesus came into the world to save sinners, of whom I am the foremost. But I received mercy for this reason, that in me, as the foremost, Jesus Christ might display his perfect patience as an example to those who were to believe in him for eternal life. To the King of the ages, immortal, invisible, the only God, be honor and glory forever and ever. Amen. (1 Timothy 1:14–17)

92

Jesus was there for me. I mailed my first card to my mom. It said "I thought of you and said a little prayer." The prayer is from the writings of Helen Farries.

> This morning when I wakened and saw the sun above, I softly said, "Good Morning, Lord—bless everyone I love!" Right away I thought of you and said a loving prayer that He would bless you specially and keep you free from care! I thought of all the happiness a day could hold in store; I wished it all for you because no one deserves it more! I felt so warm and good inside my heart was all aglow. I know God heard my prayer for you. He hears them all you know!

I wrote:

Mom,

> I've been praying for more than ten years that God would give you the will and strength

to quit drinking. I love you. Please let the people help you. Everybody cares so much about you. You're a special lady. I'll be there for you when they say I can. I'm praying for you.

Love, JoAnn

Nate loves you too!

I saved all the worksheets she was given as part of the program. One was fill in the blanks about feelings. I would like others to see me as being: "loved, optimistic, confident, appreciated."

I feel the most resentment toward: "myself—for all the hurt and harm I have caused."

I can talk about anything with: "my kids."

Most of my anger is directed toward: "me."

I wish I could get rid of this anger by: "closing the chapters on wrong doings in the past."

I feel most guilty because: "I drink."

I would like to make amends by: "apologizing to those I hurt."

It's hard for me to feel loved when: "I'm disappointed, ashamed, upset, miserable."

Those are only a sampling. My heart just breaks reading her beautiful penmanship express all of the pain she was feeling. It makes me feel good that she felt like she could talk about anything with her kids.

On the worksheet associated with step 1 of the twelve steps, it said, "Give ten reasons you need to be here." She wrote sixteen reasons. Another question was, how did you get the money to spend on alcohol? Her answer: "Lately I'd buy a couple at the bar, and friends bought the rest."

It makes me so sad. Her real friends wouldn't buy drinks for her, knowing she was in the late stages of alcoholism. But bar friends did. Her real friends had done everything they could to try to help her, but none of us could compete with the power that alcohol had over her.

Jesus is more powerful than alcoholism. But God gave us free will. Alcoholics need to choose to overcome alcoholism, and Jesus is there for them. The shortest verse in the Bible is "Jesus wept" (John 11:35). It's in the story where Jesus raises his friend Lazarus from the dead as people witnessed it so more would believe that he is the Christ, the Son of God. Jesus loved Mary, Martha, and their brother Lazarus. Jesus went back to Judea to do this, even though he knew it would be more reason for him to be persecuted. From that day on, those who feared that everyone would believe in him made plans to put him to death. Jesus loved Lazarus, and he loves each and every one of us. He wants us to believe in him so we can be raised to eternal life with him.

> So they took away the stone. And Jesus lifted up his eyes and said, "Father, I thank you that you have heard me. I knew that you always hear me, but I said this on account of the people standing around that they may believe that you sent me." When he had said these things, he cried out with a loud voice, "Lazarus, come out." The

man who had died came out, his hands and feet bound with linen strips, and his face wrapped with a cloth. Jesus said to them, "Unbind him, and let him go." (John 11:41–44)

93

On the step 1 worksheet, my mom wrote:

> I disliked telling lies to cover up my drinking. I'm determined to stop for myself—to be free from booze. I need to unconditionally surrender so my mind is clear to follow the twelve steps and let God take over. I have to decide and give myself to the program. It doesn't always work if forced to. I'll take one day at a time. How do I acquire happiness? By turning my life over to God.

On the "Problems and Goals" worksheet, she wrote:

> My most serious life problems right now other than drinking are health and financial, both caused by alcohol. It took years to deteriorate and will take years to recover. I blew a lot of money on booze and bars, money I could have spent on kids and house. I discuss my problems with my kids and family. We are a sharing and caring family. My church has a new pastor. I intend to visit him and

get back to going to church. Alcohol caused me to drift apart from God and my family. I'll keep coping with my problems daily, a fight for the rest of my life. I have no option, one drink and I'm dead. I pray for help. What's your idea of the perfect solution, what do you want? To quit drinking, trust in God and everything will fall in place.

On the step 2 worksheet, she wrote:

The treatment program has helped me and I need to continue following the twelve steps. I need help with my alcohol problem. I realize what a crutch alcohol has been. What crutch are you going to use instead of alcohol? God—by letting him take over my life. Are you keeping an open mind and praying for knowledge of God's will? Yes.

I had mailed another card to my mom. It said "Thinking of you...with love and best wishes." And I wrote:

Keep strong Mom, I know you can do it. I love you very much! Quitting drinking was the greatest gift you ever could have given. You're making my dreams come true. I'm very proud of you. My prayers are with you.

Love, JoAnn

My Mom completed a diagnostic interview with a counselor on August 17, 1990. It was a Friday. She had checked "yes" on twenty-nine of the thirty questions, so she was being very honest about how bad it was. She had been there a couple of weeks, and it wasn't yet time to allow visits by family.

Step 2 was as far as she would get in her twelve-step treatment program. As she was getting up to get ready for another day in the treatment program on Monday, August 20, she passed a lot of blood, so much that she fell down in the bathroom and cracked her head open right down to the skull. She was moved to another area in the hospital to get the care she needed. They called me right away, so I called in to work and went straight there.

She looked so ill when I got there. She was pale, weak, bloated, and uncomfortable. They were working to get her more stabilized with blood transfusions while monitoring and running tests to assess her current condition. I stayed there for the day and into the evening. The staff encouraged me to go home to get some sleep. They assured me they would monitor her closely, take great care of her, and call me if needed. I gave my mom one of my biggest hugs, told her I loved her and that I would pray for her. She whispered that she loved me too, and I cried as I walked away to go home.

Jesus was there for me. And I had utmost faith that he was there for her.

> Blessed be the God and Father of our Lord
> Jesus Christ, the Father of mercies and God of all
> comfort, who comforts us in all our affliction, so
> that we may be able to comfort those who are in

any affliction, with the comfort with which we ourselves are comforted by God. (2 Corinthians 1:3–4)

94

Nate held me in his arms as I cried when I got home. I called my brother and godmother with the end of day update. It was sure different back then with no cell phones. Nate and I went to bed, and I planned to go back to the hospital in the morning. I prayed for my mom until I fell asleep.

At 1:30 a.m., I was awakened by our phone ringing. It was the doctor providing care for my mom at the hospital. He said she was bleeding internally in volumes larger than what they were equipped to handle there. He told me she should be airlifted to Mayo in Rochester, but she didn't have any insurance. I told him I don't care if she has insurance or not, please do whatever is necessary to save her! I think I was as surprised as the doctor probably was that I was yelling.

He gave me the address for the Saint Mary's campus where she would arrive on the helicopter. He warned me that she may not make it there alive. My head was spinning as Nate and I were quickly getting ready to drive to Rochester. I called my brother. He had so many responsibilities at home. He thanked me for everything I was doing and that he'd rather get updates from me than go. I called my godmother. She said that she and her husband (my godfather) would meet us there.

We had never been to the Mayo Clinic Hospitals and getting to the right place in the dark the first time there was a challenge. I was so grateful that Nate was driving. My godparents, Nate, and I managed to get ourselves to the area where my mom was admitted about the same time. As we waited for someone to come out with an update, we were filled with anxiety, wondering if she was still alive or not.

Finally, a doctor came out to talk with us. He said she was still with us but had lost an incredible amount of blood and was continuing to bleed internally. They were giving her plasma and a plethora of other treatments. He told us a team of doctors would be put together for her care. They would complete additional testing and provide another update as soon as they could. We wouldn't be able to see her for a while yet. Then the questions came from the doctor. Who will be the decision-maker for her when she's unable?

I answered, "Me, I'm her daughter."

"If she goes code blue, meaning in cardiac or respiratory arrest, do you want us to resuscitate her?"

I thought, *O God, help me* and answered, "No." I could feel the pity from Nate and my godparents without them saying it.

I remember how close I felt to my godparents as we waited. The four of us tried to nap a little in the chairs in the waiting room. We stayed there the whole day together while my mom's care team did everything they could for her. She was bleeding heavily, and things didn't look good for her. I felt so grateful that Nate and my godparents were there for me.

More importantly, Jesus was there for me. Jesus was there for all of us. At this point in time, I had made assumptions that my mom had kept her faith throughout her alcoholism. She hadn't talked about it, and I wouldn't find her worksheets until later. I just couldn't imagine that someone who had the strong faith she did before her alcoholism could ever let it go. I prayed and prayed. As much as I wanted to have my sober mom back to live life with me going forward, I knew I needed to start praying for what was best for her. Only God would know what was best for her. She was suffering, and I didn't want that for her.

"Therefore I tell you, whatever you ask in prayer, believe that you have received it, and it will be yours" (Mark 11:24).

95

We stayed overnight in Rochester. I started making notes about my mom's condition. I didn't get any calls overnight. When we arrived in the morning the care team met with us. They introduced themselves and explained each of their unique specialties of care. I remember feeling a bit overwhelmed with the high quality of care and concern my mom was being given, even though she didn't have insurance. There was no doubt they were giving her the best of care.

But they told us their hands were tied. Mom was still heavily bleeding internally, and her pro time was unchanged at seventeen, even with four units of plasma. And to make matters worse, she was suffocating because she had aspirated blood into her lungs. They were keeping her as comfortable as possible and doing everything they could to treat her. Again, they asked me, "If she goes code blue, do you want us to resuscitate her?"

And again I said, "No."

We could go in to see her. I was so scared. I saw my beautiful mom lying there bloated, swollen, jaundiced, and suffocating. And I couldn't help but think about the power that alcoholism had on her. It was powerful enough for her to keep drinking one drink after another until this all happened.

That was the day I learned more than I care to know about pro time. The prothrombin time, sometimes referred to as PT or pro time test, is a test to evaluate blood clotting. Prothrombin is a protein produced by your liver. It is one of many factors in your blood that help it to clot appropriately. The prothrombin time test also may be performed to check for liver disease. It is one of many tests used to screen people waiting for liver transplants. That screening, known as the model for end-stage liver disease (MELD) is a scoring system for assessing the severity of chronic liver disease.

And so the waiting began. Unless her pro time would come down, there was not much more the doctors could do. We'd need to wait to find out if her pro time would come down before they could take next steps in her treatment. No more options were available if her blood would not clot appropriately. We updated my brother and my mom's other siblings. The day felt so long. We decided we would stay in Rochester another night because we wanted to be nearby in case we would get a call to have a chance to be with her in her final moments. I didn't want her to be alone when she died. I had promised I'd be there for her if and when she stopped drinking.

I prayed and prayed for what was best for my mom. I really didn't want it to end this way. I had so many questions I wanted to ask her to help me understand her perspective about her alcoholism. All I knew was my own perspective. I simply could not understand how this could have happened to her. She was the strongest person I knew, the most loving and giving mom someone could have, and she had the strongest faith in God that she taught to me and my brother. How could alcohol change all of that?

I had no doubt that Jesus was there for me. And he was there for all of us. His love never fails, and his mercy never ends. I prayed for guidance because I really didn't know what to do or how to answer the questions I was being asked. I wondered how someone could try to navigate something like this without Jesus. I would feel so alone and incapable. I was so thankful I had a relationship with Jesus, and no matter what happened, he would carry me through.

> Give thanks to the Lord, for he is good, for his steadfast love endures forever. Give thanks to the God of gods, for his steadfast love endures forever. Give thanks to the Lord of lords, for his steadfast love endures forever; to him who alone does great wonders, for his steadfast love endures forever. (Psalm 136:1–4)

96

I didn't get any calls overnight. When we arrived in the morning, we awaited the update from my mom's care team. It was a miracle! My mom's pro time was down to 13.5. This meant there were options for additional treatment. And even better, my mom was alert enough to learn about the options and make decisions for herself. I was so relieved. The best option would be for her to be put on a respirator so they could clean the fluid out of her lungs and give them a chance to heal. And they would try to stop some of the bleeding by sclerosing the varices in her esophagus. Varices are large, dilated veins that develop in the esophagus when there is elevated pressure in the portal vein, the large vein that enters the liver. This elevated pressure can occur under several circumstances, including severe liver disease.

Given all the suffering my mom had already endured, I was surprised when she decided she wanted them to proceed with their proposed treatment. I felt so bad for her. She must have been so scared. She was in pain, and it was very difficult for her to breathe with all the fluid in her lungs. Having almost suffocated to death myself the one time I rode a horse that I was allergic to, I could empathize with her fear of suffocating to death. I wondered if her choice to proceed with the treatment was to end the current fear and suffering or if she really hoped in her heart that she could recover. By now, her mind was mostly free from the grip of alcohol. I saw her wanting to fight to live.

Most of our day was spent waiting while the procedures were performed and then waiting to see her again. Once again, walking into her room was scary for me. Seeing her on a respirator along with the bloating and jaundice was really hard. Damn alcohol! I prayed for whatever would be best for my mom. We decided to stay another night in Rochester. Although she was pretty stable for the time being, the doctors made it clear she was in critical condition and still at high risk of additional internal bleeding.

The thing about alcoholism is if it goes untreated, the progression is pretty much the same for everyone. When it advances to the state it did for my mom, when the liver disease becomes severe due to years of damage from trying to filter alcohol out of your body, it's pretty dire for the alcoholic. And it's horrible for a family member to witness. I pray that if you're reading this, and you are an alcoholic or at risk of becoming an alcoholic, please know that this could happen to you.

The Alcoholics Anonymous book including the Twelve Steps was first published in 1939. The Twelve Steps were based on belief in God. There's reference to "a power greater than ourselves" for those who will still hopefully get to know God. I believe only God is powerful enough to help someone overcome alcoholism. As humans, we're limited in our ability to overcome temptations and challenges.

I cannot imagine what my life would have turned out to be if I didn't have my faith in God. I believe Jesus has been with me every day of my life, and without him, I would not be who I am today. I'm perfectly imperfect and now humbly trying to reach others in hopes they will also know and trust Jesus. Jesus was there for me. He's there for every one of us. He forgives us even though we don't deserve it. He loves us unconditionally. He yearns for us to allow him to guide us and give us joy, even when we don't feel like we can find it anywhere in this world.

> In this the love of God was made manifest among us, that God sent his only Son into the world, so that we might live through him. In this is love, not that we have loved God but that he loved us and sent his Son to be the propitiation for our sins. (1 John 4:9–10)

97

Once again, we stayed overnight in Rochester. My mom was still in critical condition in the ICU, and only time would tell if the procedures they performed would bring the results they hoped. I didn't get any calls overnight. In the morning, we awaited an update from her care team. The doctors were pleased with her progress so far and said it would be best for her to get as much rest as possible while on the respirator. It was now a Friday, and we had been there since very early Tuesday morning, except for the trips that Nate and my godfather had made to get more clothes from home.

Every day, the doctors asked me if she should be resuscitated if she went code blue. I remember wondering how that could possibly be a question I should need to answer. It was a life-and-death decision for my own mother. Who was I to make that decision? I wanted that decision to be between her and God. She didn't have anything in writing, and we had never discussed her wishes. She was forty-nine years old! I prayed that if she would die that it wouldn't have anything to do with the decision the doctors repeatedly asked me to make.

Throughout the day, we received updates that as long as my mom kept doing as well as she was, they would take the respirator off by the end of the day. It was a balancing act between giving her lungs rest to heal but not give up on working. I trusted her care team and continued to be amazed they would give her such high quality and compassionate care when she was uninsured. I didn't know anything about what was happening to her, and they would take the time to explain everything as it happened.

At 4:00 p.m. that day, they took the respirator off, and by the grace of God, she could breathe on her own well enough for the doctors to leave her off of it. The bleeding had mostly stopped as well. Her care team met with us and told us she was stable enough for us to go home. They said we could have short visits with her before we leave, but it was most important for her to get rest. They assured us they would call me if anything concerning happened and encouraged us to get rest too.

My mom was very tired and still looked so horribly ill. I could tell she didn't like having to wear the oxygen mask. She didn't like it strapped around her head and covering her nose and mouth and kept pulling on it. She was too weak to talk. I told her the doctors were encouraging us to go home so she could get good rest. We had been there all week with her, and I would be back. I said I was so sorry this was happening to her and that I would be there for her every step of the way. It was so hard for me to say goodbye and leave, but I held her hand, said "I love you, Mom," and left her room.

Jesus was there for me. And I knew he was there for her. I pictured Jesus at her bedside, and I felt him with me. He's there for you too. He's there for every one of us all the time, through the good and through the bad. I felt so grateful that my parents introduced me to Jesus and nurtured the growth of my faith when I was a child. What a gift it is to have someone love you enough to make sure you have the opportunity to get to know Jesus. When I became a parent, I knew the most important thing I could do for my daughters was to introduce them to Jesus and nurture the growth of their faith. I believe that with Jesus, everything else in life can be handled.

"But to all who did receive him, who believed in his name, he gave the right to become children of God" (John 1:12).

98

On that Saturday morning, I waited for the update from my mom's care team by phone. They had made it pretty clear that unless something changed for the worse, it would really be best for my mom to be able to rest and not have visitors. Although it was hard to stay home, I had to admit it felt good to get caught up on some things and just be home again. I had witnessed her care team provide the best of care for her and had no doubt they would continue to do the same while I was home.

None of us had any idea how long she'd need to be hospitalized or what her future would hold. I didn't have options to take a "family leave" from work then like I do now. I'd need to return to work and visit my mom after work and on weekends. The Mayo Hospital was one hour and twenty minutes from my home and in the opposite direction from work. My commute to work was forty minutes one way. I talked with Nate about this. It would mean I wouldn't see much of him, and he'd need to take care of everything at home while I was gone, except for short nights of sleep. I felt so strongly that I needed to be there for my mom. I had promised her I'd be there if she quit drinking, and I had a feeling the number of days I had left with her were limited.

I got a good night of sleep, and when her care team called on that Sunday morning, they said her condition was improving and they were going to have her start trying to drink fluids. I updated my brother and godmother. Her care team said it would be okay for her close family to come for short visits. I went to spend the day at the hospital again, knowing I'd need to return to work the next day after being out the whole week before.

Her care team explained their assessment for her future. The bleeding varices in her esophagus could start bleeding again. She might develop pneumonia given all the stress on her lungs. And only time would tell if her liver function would improve or deteriorate. And there was risk of bleeding in other areas. Because her liver was barely functioning, fluid was backing up in her abdomen, putting pressure and stress on her whole digestive system that was already damaged from alcohol. So, basically, it sounded to me like it would take a miracle for her to live through this.

Jesus was there for me. And Jesus was there for her. I wanted to pray for a miracle, but with the suffering she was already enduring, I knew I needed to pray for what was best for her. My mom was able to drink fluids for the first time in a week and her mind was clear, so I had my loving sober mom back. She was clearly suffering, but I think she was as happy as I was that we could have the opportunity to start talking like a mom and daughter would again. I let her know I'd need to get back to work, but I would visit after work and on the weekends, and she was grateful. My mom, when not numbed by alcohol, had never asked for much for herself and was always grateful for what she was given. My mom was freed from alcohol but sadly not from the damage it had done.

> Finally, brothers, whatever is true, whatever is honorable, whatever is just, whatever is pure, whatever is lovely, whatever is commendable, if there is any excellence, if there is anything worthy of praise, think about these things. What you have learned and received and heard and seen in me—practice these things, and the God of peace will be with you. (Philippians 4:8–9)

99

Returning to work was difficult. I wanted to be at the hospital, and because of that, I couldn't focus at work. I had given my mom's care team my work phone number, but I felt so nervous while in my car or even to step away from my desk. Back then, without cell phones, I was unreachable when not by a phone with one of the numbers I'd given to her care team. I began receiving weekday morning updates on my phone at work. My friends at work were all so supportive of me and were praying for my mom.

The first update I got at work was a good one. My mom would be moved out of ICU and into a regular room. I couldn't wait to get there. This meant I could visit with her without limitations on length of stay. Although my day was busy catching up on work from having been gone for a week, the day couldn't go fast enough. Finally, I was on my way to Rochester again. When I arrived, I found the new room my mom was in.

She didn't have any IVs because her care team felt that pushing fluids was only making her bloat worse, and she was able to drink fluids on her own. She was finally able to get rid of the oxygen mask that bothered her. They had switched to oxygen by nose only. And, unfortunately, she had developed pneumonia which they were treating. I stayed pretty late that night because I wanted every minute of precious time with my sober loving mom. I didn't want to pressure her with all my questions but rather just enjoy good conversation with her now that her mind was clear.

I assured her I'd be with her as much as possible while keeping up on my responsibilities at work. I reminded her that I had promised to be there for her if she quit drinking, and I was going to keep my promise. In my mind, I thought this wasn't at all how I had hoped to be there for her. I had hoped she would realize she should get help to stop drinking before her health declined this badly. But at the same time, I was grateful for this time with her. For me, it would have been worse to get a call that she had passed before I would get time with her sober again.

I told her I loved her very much and then made the journey back home for a short sleep. Then back to work. The morning update was mostly more of the same. The only thing new was they were getting concerned about how much fluid was building up because her liver wasn't working well. The more bloat, the more pressure on the varices, and increased risk for more bleeding. Another day at work finally ended, and back to Rochester I went. She was very bloated in her abdomen and swollen everywhere. Even without IVs, her body wasn't able to function properly, and fluid was backing up because her liver wasn't working.

Her care team said they'd need to start taking fluid out of her abdomen by inserting a needle to extract the fluid using a syringe. The excess fluid in the abdomen is called ascites. The most common cause is cirrhosis, and the procedure to remove the excess fluid is called paracentesis. The removal of several liters of fluid would decrease the pressure and pain. I felt so bad for my mom. She was suffering so much. The grip of alcohol had so much control over her that she ended up like this. I wondered how awful she must have felt for a long time as her liver was failing. She had complained about being overweight, apparently not making the connection that her belly was getting larger from her liver failing. And one drink at a time, it had continued.

Jesus was there for me and for her. Together, we were learning things we never knew and taking one day at time.

"You then, my child, be strengthened by the grace that is in Christ Jesus" (2 Timothy 2:1).

100

I had been given the opportunity to ask my mom how she would answer the question I was being asked by the doctors. She said she was giving the same answer as me. If she went code blue, she did not want to be resuscitated. I was so grateful I was able to ask her for her answer and not need to make that decision on my own.

The next morning, I received an update that she was bleeding heavily again. They would need to try to stop some of the bleeding by sclerosing the varices in her esophagus again. And perhaps additional treatments would be needed. I left work and headed to Rochester. When I got there, I learned they also had to put a balloon in her stomach in an effort to stop bleeding there. The balloon could be expanded to put pressure on bleeds to stop them and then be deflated when not needed. That sounded just absolutely horrible to me. My mom was put back into ICU. She was exhausted from everything that was happening to her.

Jesus was there for her. And Jesus was there for me. I couldn't believe everything she was going through as she was fighting for her life. Per the worksheets she had completed in treatment, in her opinion, it had been twelve years since she lost control of her life to alcohol. I cannot imagine going through this journey with my mom without Jesus and the hope and promise of eternal life.

At the time I'm writing this, today is Christmas Eve, the eve of the birth of our Lord and Savior Jesus Christ. I've written a hundred entries since Easter. I guess some people write books in a couple of weeks. I felt called by God to write about Jesus in my life. Knowing I couldn't do it on my own, I asked him to work through me and for his words to flow through me. I trust God's timing, even if it means I was awake at 1:30 a.m., making notes because the words started flowing at that time today.

Who or what do you worship? We all worship someone or something. One definition of worship is to show a lot of love and adoration for someone or something. We tend to give our time and attention to what or who we worship.

If you died today, what would that someone or something do for you? Would your sins be forgiven and all your wrongs made right? Where do you believe you will go when you die? Is your heart filled with contentment? Or is something still missing? Are you in a storm and just wish someone would calm the storm and give you peace?

The more I write, the more humbled I am by how Jesus really is always there for me. He gives me everything I need. There is no promise that life will be easy. It's not, and that's why we need Jesus. I could end the story here with all honor and glory going to Jesus. But there is more to tell.

Jesus is there for you. If you haven't already accepted Jesus as your Lord and Savior, please consider it. He wants nothing more than to have a relationship with you. Accept the greatest gift ever given. His love never fails.

"For to us a child is born, to us a son is given; and the government shall be upon his shoulder, and his name shall be called Wonderful Counselor, Mighty God, Everlasting Father, Prince of Peace" (Isaiah 9:6).

101

Once again, my mom's care team advised me it would be best for them to help her get as much rest as possible for her body to heal. Her brothers, sisters, and other family members wanted to get a chance to see her, but with all the ups and downs and time in ICU, they would need to wait and hope they'd get an opportunity.

The next day, I received another update from her care team. She had a slight fever, and her blood pressure had plummeted to 70/? (I couldn't remember the diastolic number they told me when I wrote my notes). They had put an IV lead in her neck. They weren't able to use the veins in her arms because they weren't viable. They thought her blood pressure drop was from not having enough fluid versus bleeding because they weren't seeing any bleeding. The balloon was deflated but still in her stomach in case bleeding would start again. They were having to do a juggling act to give her enough fluids to maintain her blood pressure while remaining concerned about the pressure from fluid building up in her abdomen with her liver not working.

I felt so bad for her. She was suffering so much. At this point, I started feeling regret for not honoring her wishes to be left to die in her bed at home. I felt guilty and selfish. She'd been in the hospital for ten days, and it was like torture for her. I realize it wasn't feasible for me to have let her lie in her bed and die at home. I was terrified about what she would have gone through without medical care, and I wouldn't have been able to just leave her there alone. But this was so difficult. Damn alcohol!

I had started mourning the loss of my mom years before her flight to Mayo. We had lost her to alcohol, and since having my seizure, I hadn't seen her more than a few times in nearly two years. This was a whole new level of suffering the wrath of alcoholism. There really seemed like there was no hope for her to recover from this, and I didn't want her to suffer. I'm sure she had been suffering in the grip of alcohol for many years in all kinds of ways that I simply wouldn't be able to understand.

Although it was way worse for Job in the Bible, Job 30:24–27 describes what it felt like.

> Yet does not one in a heap of ruins stretch
> out his hand, and in his disaster cry for help? Did
> not I weep for him whose day was hard? Was not
> my soul grieved for the needy? But when I hoped
> for good, evil came, and when I waited for light,
> darkness came. My inward parts are in turmoil
> and never still; days of affliction come to meet me.

Jesus was there for me, and he was there for her. I prayed for whatever would be best for her. I prayed for her care team to do what was best for her. I didn't know what would be best. I had to put my trust in God. The only thing I was sure about was that I would keep my promise to her. She had quit drinking, and I would be there for her.

With Jesus there is always hope, always help, and always comfort. It may not come in the way you think or at the time you hope. If we aren't willing to trust him, we can choose to only look at what we think is betrayal or undue suffering. If we trust him, we can begin to learn he will work in ways we may not understand, and it is us that need to seek more wisdom and accept that there are things that will surpass our understanding. The Bible is the source of truth and wisdom we seek.

"He who did not spare his own Son but gave him up for us all, how will he not also with him graciously give us all things?" (Romans 8:32).

102

By the weekend, my mom's condition had stabilized, and by the end of the weekend, she was moved out of ICU and started drinking fluids again. I was able to visit with her on both weekend days. I asked her, "How did this happen?"

And she replied that she didn't know. She said at some point along the way, it started to consume her mind, and all she could think about is where and when she could have her next drink. She didn't know how she ended up making alcohol more important than everything else in her life.

She said she had so many regrets, guilt, and shame. She asked if I could forgive her. I told her that I forgave her. And I explained how I had done a lot of research about alcoholism and understood it's a disease. I just wish it was a disease that the person with it would want to recover from it. I told her it scared me that if someone like her could be overcome by it, then anyone could. I assured her that she was the most loving and giving mom I could have ever had before alcohol took control. I thanked her for helping me to grow my faith. I told her I was so sorry she was going through so much suffering, but I appreciated this time with her sober again.

A couple of definitions of *repent* are "to turn from sin and dedicate oneself to the amendment of one's life, to feel regret or contrition, to change one's mind." Jesus often answered questions or diffi-cult predicaments with a single parable or with a clear statement of truth. Luke 15 is the only place recorded in the gospels where Jesus tells three parables to emphasize one fact. First, the parable of the sheep ending with verse 7, "Just so, I tell you, there will be more joy in heaven over one sinner who repents than over ninety-nine righteous persons who need no repentance." Second, the parable of the lost coin ending with verse 10, "Just so, I tell you, there is joy before the angels of God over one sinner who repents." Third, the parable of the prodigal son ending with verse 32, "It was fitting to celebrate and be glad, for this your brother was dead, and is alive; he was lost, and is found."

Whenever you have something of great value and lose it, you search for it until you find it. You are of great value to Jesus, and if you are lost, he is searching for you. Everyone matters to God, so much so that he gave us his only Son, Jesus, to die for the forgiveness of our sins. And God asks each one of us to be the one he uses to lead someone to Jesus. I've prayed for many years for God to work through me. Feeling called to write this book is one of the bigger ways he's using me, and I hope to lead someone to Jesus. If you are lost, let yourself be found so you too can feel the strength, love, and peace that can only be found in Jesus.

Jesus was there for me, and I know he always will be. He was there for my mom. She led me and my brother to Jesus, she got lost in the grip of alcohol, she repented and was found. And I believe there was great joy in heaven. I felt great joy in having my sober mom again, but it came at great cost to her in her suffering. I hope she understood what a great gift she was giving me to have that precious time with her. I felt confident we both understood what a great gift God had given us—Jesus was there for us.

"And without faith it is impossible to please him, for whoever would draw near to God must believe that he exists and that he rewards those who seek him" (Hebrews 11:6).

103

Monday was Labor Day, so I was able to spend the day with my mom for the third day in a row. When I arrived, she had a terrible rash all over her body, and her bloat was causing her a lot of pain. She was absolutely miserable. My heart just broke for her. I cannot even imagine all the suffering she was going through. I wanted so badly for her care team to be able to do more for her, but I had to trust that with her being at Mayo with some of the world's best doctors that they were doing everything they could. I prayed and prayed for God to work through them and to do what was best for my mom.

I didn't feel like there was much hope for her to get through her suffering and into recovery. Her liver was all but completely failed. At the time, there were no machines that could do the functions of the liver like dialysis does for kidneys. One of the functions of the liver is to get rid of harmful substances from your body. My mom was suffering from the effects of liver failure and was very tired. It was really hard to leave that night. I felt so helpless and didn't know if she'd make it another day.

I had to get back to work the next day. Her care team gave me the update that they took four liters of fluid out of her abdomen, mostly blood. With that, the numbers of her liver function improved slightly. They also took out the lead in her neck. After work, I drove to Rochester again to spend time with her. She was feeling so much regret for ending up in this condition. She was so exhausted from everything she was going through. We were both in a state of feeling like "I don't know." We didn't know what to expect next or how we ended up in the place where we were.

Earlier in my book, I shared the parable Jesus told about the wise man who built his house on the foundation of a rock and the foolish man who built his house on sand as told in the book of Matthew, chapter 7. It teaches us to build our lives upon God's Word. The same parable is found in Luke, chapter 6. My Lord and Savior Jesus Christ is my firm foundation. My faith in him is unshakable. When I listen to his Word and try to do his will, my life always goes better.

I chose to be baptized in February of 2019. I had been baptized as an infant, and while still a child, I made a decision to follow Christ. Many years later, I joined a church that encourages baptism for everyone who has made a decision to follow Christ. I learned that baptism is an act of obedience and public profession of my faith in Jesus and my commitment to him. Jesus himself was baptized. Jesus was there for me my whole life, and he always will be. During my baptism, the song by Pat Barrett, "Build my Life," was played. It was based on the parable found in Matthew and Luke. It's "my song." Some of my favorite lyrics are "We live for you," "Lead me in your love to those around me," and "I will put my trust in you alone and I will not be shaken."

Why do you call me "Lord, Lord," and not do what I tell you? Everyone who comes to me and hears my words and does them, I will show you what he is like: he is like a man building a house, who dug deep and laid the foundation on the rock. And when a flood arose, the stream broke against that house and could not shake it, because it had been well built. But the one who hears and does not do them is like a man who built a house on the ground without a foundation. When the stream broke against it, immediately it fell, and the ruin of that house was great. (Luke 6:46–49)

104

The next day was the day when my mom's care team at St. Mary's told her they couldn't do anything more for her there, and she would need to move to the Methodist campus at Mayo. Her bloat had come back worse, and she was in a lot of pain. She needed a liver transplant or she'd die.

We went from not knowing what to expect next to being in shock about the reality of where she was at. I drove to Rochester after work. I remember walking into St. Mary's with so many thoughts. I felt so sad for my mom and how much she was suffering. I wondered how she felt about the news she had been given. It felt surreal that it would be the last time I'd be walking into the hospital as our sixteen-day journey there would be ending.

I had to assist my mom with paperwork necessary for her to move to the Methodist hospital the next day. She was so miserable. We were given a lot of information about the transplant evaluation process. They would begin her evaluation when she arrived at the Methodist hospital. There were strict criteria regarding eligibility. Deep down, I wondered how on earth an alcoholic like my mom would be eligible. She had only quit drinking when she got to the point that she was bleeding internally and literally couldn't drink anymore.

At the same time, I was hopeful. I thought if they were willing to evaluate her for a liver transplant, then there must be a chance that they'd determine she was eligible. Now that her mind was clear, she wanted to fight to live. She realized how alcohol had been holding her hostage, and she had finally broken free from it. But I was scared and so nervous for her. She was suffering so badly and in so much pain. Would she be able to survive long enough to go through the whole liver transplant process? She'd need a donor. Would I be a match?

We had taken a turn on our journey together, and the road had narrowed to only two paths. Which way we would go next depended upon whether or not she would be eligible for a transplant. Jesus was there for me and there for my mom. He was beside us every step of the way. And there were times I felt him carry me or lessen the load I was carrying. I tried really hard to not carry it all myself. I needed to remain strong for my mom and couldn't do that on my own.

Jesus is there for you. He loves us perfectly, even though we are imperfect. Have you ever tried to feel Jesus? Physically, we can't touch him, but I imagine what it must have been like for the people who were able to touch Jesus and talk with him when he was a man walking on this earth. It must have been amazing to watch him perform miracles. He died on a cross, was buried, and three days later rose from the dead. Many of the people who told others about Jesus when he was alive were thought to be crazy. And even more crazy were those who told others about Jesus Christ who rose from the grave, walked on earth again, and then ascended into heaven.

Some people think I'm crazy, too, to believe that Jesus is there for me. I feel Jesus. I feel him in the hard times, and I need to remember to feel him in the good times. I thank God for Jesus. For ages and ages before Jesus, God used what I think of as tough love to try to teach people to do his will. Then knowing our sinful nature and extent of our imperfections, he gave us Jesus to pay the price for our sins. We need to believe and accept the perfect gift.

"For there is one God, and there is one mediator between God and men, the man Christ Jesus, who gave himself as a ransom for all, which is the testimony given at the proper time" (1 Timothy 2:5–6).

105

My mom was moved to the Methodist hospital at Mayo, and evaluations for a liver transplant began. Part of the evaluation process was an exhaustive list of questions, much like an interview. Given her alcoholism, there were additional evaluation questions that needed to be answered. One, of course, being how long since your last drink. The answer was two months.

I remember feeling like I went to battle at that point. I don't remember all the details, but I remember having multiple meetings with the folks conducting the evaluation for my mom where I repeatedly made the case that my mom truly wanted to stay sober and fight for her life. They explained it's difficult to get approval for a liver transplant for someone who has liver failure due to alcoholism. I doubt that these were the words they used, but what I heard them say was, "We wouldn't want to waste a precious organ by giving it to someone who may destroy it."

I understood what they were saying and their obligation to conduct objective and accurate assessments, but the candidate wasn't their own mother. I was clearly fully emotionally invested while they needed to be objective. I was fighting for my mom's life, and they were obligated to make sure the most eligible candidates became recipients. I'm determined and stubborn and would guess I nearly drove them crazy. I think I made it difficult for them to remain objective while sitting in front of me with my relentless emotional pleas.

Throughout those several days, my mom remained stable. They were removing fluid from her abdomen as needed and doing everything they could to keep her as comfortable as possible. I was able to spend a lot of time with her. And much of her family was able to visit her as well. I took a break from being at the hospital on the day that was my dad's birthday. I always tried to spend time with my dad on the day of his birthday. I knew that lots of my mom's family would be there to visit her that day, and it was a nice mental break for me that was much needed.

The next day was a Sunday, so I was able to spend the entire day with my mom as well as with those who visited that day. She was doing pretty well compared to how she had been doing. I would suspect the hope for a liver transplant was having an impact on her overall well-being. We were all praying and praying. I believe in miracles. I've noticed that small miracles happen daily if I pay attention. My mom being determined eligible and surviving a liver transplant would be a huge miracle.

Waiting and wondering was hard. This was just the first step—to determine if she was eligible for a liver transplant. I learned a lot about the liver from what were some of the best liver specialists in the world there at Mayo. It's even possible to do a living-donor liver transplant. A portion of the liver from a healthy living person is removed and placed into someone whose liver is no longer working properly. The donor's remaining liver regrows and returns to its normal size, volume, and capacity.

At the same time, the transplanted liver portion grows and restores normal liver function in the recipient. There was no doubt in my mind that I would be willing to do that for my mom if it would be an option.

Jesus was there for me. And Jesus was there for my mom. Love never fails. Love for our children and love for our parents is powerful. Even when we may not like them or what they do, most times, love remains even when we may not want it to. Feeling that kind of powerful love pales in comparison to the love that Jesus has for us. We can run but we cannot hide from it. He loves us unconditionally, even if we don't believe he exists.

"Above all, keep loving one another earnestly, since love covers a multitude of sins" (1 Peter 4:8).

106

On September 10, 1990, my mom was told she was eligible for a liver transplant! She was scheduled to go to Madison in four days, and the process could begin! I couldn't believe it. I was so happy. We only had two paths to take, and this was the path for saving her life. My mind started racing with all the thoughts about what would be happening next. Could I be a donor? Or my brother? Or maybe one of her six siblings? What would this mean for my job and getting time off to go to Madison with her? How long would the whole process take, and would she survive that long?

I made my update phone calls to my brother and godmother quicker than I ever had before. They were as excited and relieved as I was. We were entering into a whole new leg of the journey, and it was one filled with hope for her recovery. It was a miracle, thank God!

Jesus performed many miracles. Matthew, chapter 8, tells us about several of them. Verses 14–17 tells us how Jesus healed many.

> And when Jesus entered Peter's house, he saw his mother-in-law lying sick with a fever. He touched her hand, and the fever left her, and she rose and began to serve him. That evening they brought to him many who were oppressed by

demons, and he cast out the spirits with a word and healed all who were sick. This was to fulfill what was spoken by the prophet Isaiah: "He took our illnesses and bore our diseases."

The miracle I love most from Matthew, chapter 8, is when Jesus calmed a storm. Jesus calms our storms if we let him. I have clung to this miracle from the first time I read it. When bad things happen, even people who don't yet know Jesus search for something or someone to lean on to help them get through the hard times. People turn to prayer and churches when bad things happen. Evil things happen in this world because Satan is still trying to win the souls of God's people. People have free will, and they can choose. I choose Jesus. He is my rock on which I stand, and he calms my storms.

As everyone does, I receive feedback from people in my personal life and people I work with. The most common and consistent bit of feedback is that I'm calm and have a calming effect on others. I'm sought out by people who need to be calmed down. I do not take credit for being calm. I give all honor and glory to God that I have learned how to be calm and calm others from Jesus. I am human, and my ability to be calm and have a calming effect pales in comparison to the calm that Jesus gives. And Jesus is there for every one of us all at the same time! Jesus was there for me. He is there for you. There's always room for growth in our faith. Please join me, if you haven't already, to continue to learn and grow your faith in Jesus Christ.

And when he got into the boat, his disciples followed him. And behold, there arose a great storm on the sea, so that the boat was being swamped by the waves; but he was asleep. And they went and woke him, saying, "Save us, Lord; we are perishing." And he said to them, "Why are you afraid, O you of little faith?" Then he rose and rebuked the winds and the sea, and there was a great calm. And the men marveled, saying, "What sort of man is this, that even winds and sea obey him?" (Matthew 8:23–27)

107

The next day, there was confusion about my mom going to Madison. I'll never know the specifics of the confusion, but we were being told she may not be eligible for a liver transplant. We didn't know either way for the whole day. After being so happy and relieved that there was hope for us taking the path for saving her life, we were back to the fork in the road. We had barely taken a step in the direction we had hoped to go.

I couldn't believe it! How did we go from being told she's eligible for a liver transplant and a scheduled move to the hospital in Madison where it would be done to "I don't know" again? I was so angry and disheartened. Why, why, why? I had to call and update my brother and godmother. Everyone who loved my mom, excited by the news the day before, would be let down again.

I was so sad for my mom. I felt like together we had won a battle in her fight to live and in no time at all, we didn't know if that was still true. And we weren't getting any answers about what was being questioned or why there was confusion. My mom and I talked a lot during my visit after work that day. I stayed as late as I could, hoping we'd get some answers, but we didn't get any. We'd need to wait until the next day and hope for answers then. The drive home felt really long that night. This was our last hope, and it felt like it was fading away.

Jesus was there for me, my mom, and everyone who loved her. I prayed all the way home. God knows my every thought and feeling. I prayed for what I wanted, which was for my mom to be able to continue her fight to live. But then I prayed for what was best for her. God only knew that, not me. She had made decisions with her free will. People had created policies regarding transplant eligibility. Qualified individuals had conducted their assessment, and decisions were made. And those decisions were being reconsidered. God gave all people free will, and we all make decisions. Those decisions impact ourselves and others.

I wanted control! And I had none. I cannot even imagine how God and Jesus feel watching us make our decisions with free will as a Father and Friend wanting only the very best for us. The devil constantly tempts us with appealing ways to sin. When we make bad decisions, we suffer the consequences. First Peter 5:8–11 tells us:

> Be sober-minded; be watchful. Your adversary the devil prowls around like a roaring lion, seeking someone to devour. Resist him, firm in your faith, knowing that the same kinds of suffering are being experienced by your brotherhood throughout the world. And after you have suffered a little while, the God of all grace, who has called you to his eternal glory in Christ, will himself restore, confirm, strengthen, and establish you. To him be the dominion forever and ever. Amen.

Our Father God and Friend Jesus are always there for us. We are never alone. And we can never fall too far away from God's grace. Jesus died for the forgiveness of our sins. We're given his grace, even though we don't deserve it. We need to believe Jesus and humbly receive it.

> Greater love has no one than this, that someone lay down his life for his friends. You are my friends if you do what I command you. No longer do I call you servants, for the servant does not know what his master is doing; but I have called you friends, for all that I have heard from my Father I have made known to you. (John 15:13–15)

108

The next day, it was confirmed. My mom was not eligible for a liver transplant. The reason we were given was that six months of sobriety was required for an alcoholic to be eligible for a liver transplant, and my mom only had two. I wished we would have lied about the length of her sobriety. And I'll always wonder if that was the real reason. It was known throughout the eligibility determination process that her length of sobriety was two months. She didn't have medical insurance, so I couldn't help but wonder if that had anything to do with it. No matter the reason, we were once again on one path, and it wasn't the one we had hoped for.

My mom's condition had remained stable, and I believe it had a lot to do with the hope of a potential liver transplant. She was allowed to start eating solids for the first time in over three weeks, and she was even able to take short walks. Hope is a powerful state of mind. I treasure the hope I have because of Jesus. Romans 8:24–25 tells us, "For in this hope we were saved. Now hope that is seen is not hope. For who hopes for what he sees? But if we hope for what we do not see, we wait for it with patience."

I believe that even if we don't receive what we hoped for here on earth, with Jesus, we have hope that we will live a perfect eternal life with him when we die. Without Jesus, we will not.

By the end of the day, my mom was diagnosed with pneumonia again. What a roller coaster we were on! I was exhausted from it all and wasn't the one suffering like my mom was. I cannot even imagine the extent of her pain and suffering and the psychological and emotional turmoil she was going through. We didn't know what to expect going forward, other than the most likely outcome was that she would bleed to death. We didn't know how much time she had left or how it would go. One thing was clear: we were on the final leg of her journey. I don't remember my mom telling me how she felt at that point, but I remember her being quiet. I was devastated and scared.

The most important thing was Jesus was there for her. Jesus was there for me. His grace is sufficient. Her body was ravaged from what started as a decision made with her free will to drink alcohol to alcoholism taking control and destroying her life. But because she believed in Jesus and accepted his gift of forgiveness of her sins, her soul would be saved. She had introduced me to Jesus and helped me grow my faith. I would find strength and be blessed with everything I needed to go on living my life. Because of Jesus, we both had hope.

> So we do not lose heart. Though our outer self is wasting away, our inner self is being renewed day by day. For this light momentary affliction is preparing for us an eternal weight of glory beyond all comparison, as we look not to the things that are seen but to the things that are unseen. For the things that are seen are transient, but the things that are unseen are eternal. (2 Corinthians 4:16–18)

109

The very next day, my mom was put back in the ICU. She had passed blood for the first time in a while. They put a scope down her throat again and determined the bleeding was not from the varices. Her hope for a liver transplant was gone. She was very depressed when I got there after work that day. She felt so much regret. Even she herself could not understand how the grip of alcoholism had become so powerful that it had taken control of her and was killing her. That is scary! It could happen to anyone, and it does.

What would it feel like to know you were going to die within days, weeks, or months? Maybe you are someone who has been given a time "limit" here on earth. Or maybe you know someone who has. We all know we're going to die, but I wonder what it must feel like to know it is imminent within a short period of time. Having watched my parents and my parents-in-law all experience that, I've given it thought. My conclusion is that I cannot know how I would actually feel until if and when it happens to me.

The most important question is, where will you go when you die? What will happen to you after you die? The Bible tells us there's two options. Both are eternal—a loving home in heaven or a burning lake of fire in hell. Jesus alone is the difference. We can't earn our way into heaven and we can't save ourselves from hell. Do you believe and put your trust in Jesus?

If you don't believe the Bible, I encourage you to read it and learn more. One good thing that has come with the Internet is the ability to search for topics in the Bible. You quickly realize that no matter what you search for, there are pages of verses from different books related to the topic. Even though the Bible was written over more than a thousand years by many authors on different continents and in different languages, it has an extensive network of what we now call hyperlinks throughout the books of the Bible. How could that be if what's written in the Bible isn't true?

If you're willing to gamble, what would be the better bet? Learning to trust Jesus and gamble on eternal life in heaven with him? Or ignoring everything related to Jesus and gamble on eternal life burning in a lake of fire? Or maybe you're someone who thinks you'll fade away to nothingness when you die and are willing to gamble on that?

Where is your hope? Why would anyone make the choice to try to navigate this world alone without Jesus, given all the evil temptations, struggles, and pain? I am weak. I am a sinner. I get lost. I make mistakes. I make bad choices. I hurt others. I've hurt myself. I'm human just like everyone else. Without Jesus, I would have given up as a teenager and would have acted on my suicidal thoughts. Jesus was there for me. He's always there for me and for you!

The more I learn about Jesus, the closer to him I feel. I trust him to guide me in my life here on earth, and when I die, I believe I'll go to the heavenly home he's prepared for me. I'll be reunited with everyone I love who went there before me. And when I'm there, I'll welcome everyone who comes after me. For now, I'm humbly trying to tell others about Jesus. That's what is asked of me. My hope is in him. To him be all the glory!

"But in your hearts honor Christ the Lord as holy, always being prepared to make a defense to anyone who asks you for a reason for the hope that is in you; yet do it with gentleness and respect" (1 Peter 3:15).

110

The next day, they kept my mom in the ICU to keep a close watch on her. She passed more blood, so they gave her two units of blood. She was still depressed, tired, and clearly did not feel well at all. It was so hard to see her suffering like she was. I wished that there was something that could be done to help her. Most of my stay was spent holding her hand in silence. We were both deep in thought, and it felt good just being with her. I knew my time with her was running out, and it was really hard to leave her that night. It was a Friday, so I stayed a little later and promised I'd spend the whole weekend with her, except to go home to sleep.

That was the first time I experienced being by the side of someone who was dying. I loved my mom, and my heart was broken. I didn't really know what to think. I was sad that for half of my life with my mom, it was tumultuous because of her alcoholism. I was angry that alcoholism had taken control of her life. I was frustrated that it was too late to be able to do anything to help her recover from the damage that had been done. I was scared because I didn't know what to expect to happen going forward. And I mourned all the things my mom wouldn't be there with me for in the future. But I knew I'd keep my promise to be there for her until the end of her life.

Psalm 34:18 tells us "The LORD is near to the brokenhearted and saves the crushed in spirit."

Jesus was there for me and he was there for my mom. He would help us get through whatever was going to happen. His love never fails. He loves us, walks beside us, and carries us from the beginning of our life to the end, even if we don't acknowledge him. Romans 8:37–39 tells us:

> No, in all these things we are more than conquerors through him who loved us. For I am sure that neither death nor life, nor angels nor rulers, nor things present nor things to come, nor powers, nor height nor depth, nor anything else in all creation, will be able to separate us from the love of God in Christ Jesus our Lord.

Jesus loves my mom, he loves me, and he loves you. He loves us just as we are. He yearns for a relationship with us and for us to believe in him and trust him. We may not be able to understand the kind of love he has for us because we're not capable of it. We likely wouldn't be willing to die a horrific death on a cross for the forgiveness of sins committed by others. Only Jesus. My mom and I needed Jesus, and he was there. We were weary and we needed Jesus. I still need Jesus and I always will. Do you need Jesus? He's there for you.

"Come to me, all who labor and are heavy laden, and I will give you rest. Take my yoke upon you, and learn from me, for I am gentle and lowly in heart, and you will find rest for your souls. For my yoke is easy, and my burden is light" (Matthew 11:28–30).

111

When I went to my mom's room in the ICU that Saturday morning, there were all kinds of things happening. She had bled again, quite a lot, so they did an emergency test to try to find the source of the bleeding. She was bleeding from all over her intestines. They needed to give her four units of blood. This was a devastating development. She had been bleeding in her esophagus, stomach, and intestines. So what did this mean? She bleeds and they give her blood? They had been able to control the bleeding in the esophagus by sclerosing the varices. They had been able to control the bleeding in her stomach with the balloon that they could expand to apply pressure. But how would they be able to stop bleeding from all over her intestines? They couldn't.

It had been only five days since they had told her she was eligible for a liver transplant and four days since they changed the determination to not eligible. If they had proceeded with the determination that she was eligible, this would have been the day she was scheduled to transfer to Madison for the transplant. In those five days, everything had changed. I stayed the whole day and into the night with her in the ICU. She continued to receive incredible care. They kept doing their best to keep her comfortable. She slept quite a bit, exhausted from everything she had gone through.

Like most of my long drives home from the hospital, I talked and prayed to God. Jesus was there for me, and I could feel him so close to me. I was still feeling a will to fight and not give up. I didn't want my mom to die. And yet how could I expect her to go through much more? I would feel sorry for myself, thinking about how hard it was for me until I put my focus on my mom, where it belonged. It was horrible for her. And I couldn't stop thinking about the power of alcohol. Alcohol was the cause of all of it. I was having a very hard time accepting the reality of my mom's condition.

As I've written each entry in my book, I've been careful to check that I'm not referencing the same Bible verse that I've used before. When I wrote the previous entry, I included three Bible verses (which I haven't often done). I finished writing the previous entry while I was away from home. When I returned home, I failed to do my check to see if I referenced Bible verses that I already used before I posted it. I remembered to check while writing this entry. I had referenced all three verses before! The condensed version of the three verses is this: "The Lord is near, nothing can separate us from His love, and He gives us rest." This pretty much sums up my needs throughout my journey with my mom and her alcoholism. Jesus was there, and he provides for my needs.

This is the type of thing I've learned to notice. God works in mysterious ways, in small and big ways. Every time I've acted to try to do good works that I feel God has called me to do, I have learned more and more how he provides. I taught Sunday school and confirmation for sixteen years. When giving my time to teach young people about Jesus, I learned so much more myself. When helping or giving to others, we get so much more in return. First Peter 4:10 tells us, "As each has received a gift, use it to serve one another, as good stewards of God's varied grace."

I pray this book will help someone. While writing, I'm learning, healing, and feeling humbled more every day by how God is working through my life experience to make the words flow out onto the pages. All glory and praise to him!

"Therefore, my beloved brothers, be steadfast, immovable, always abounding in the work of the Lord, knowing that in the Lord your labor is not in vain" (1 Corinthians 15:58).

112

When I arrived at the hospital that Sunday morning, I walked into my mom's room, and her bed was empty! Oh no! I ran to the desk in a panic. "Where is my mom? What happened?" The seconds or minutes it took felt like a really long time.

The nurse explained my mom had been moved out of the ICU and to a room on another floor. I went as quickly as I could because that was all the information I had.

I walked into my mom's room. It was very empty and quiet. As I approached my mom's bedside. She looked at me and said, "Thy will be done." I paused and tried to gather my thoughts while I looked into her eyes. She told me the doctors had explained to her there was nothing more they could do for her. She had made the decision to stop taking blood because it would only prolong the inevitable. Her understanding was that she would fall asleep as she bled to death, timing unknown.

I hugged her and told her that I understood. I wasn't ready for it, but I would be there for her until the end. Throughout the rest of the day, she told me everything I'd need to do when she was gone. Jesus was there for me and for my mom.

"Thy will be done" is a phrase likely everyone has at least heard. The Lord's Prayer is found in Matthew 6 and Luke 11. It's the prayer

Jesus teaches us to pray. His instructions are to not heap up empty phrases because our Father knows what we need before we ask him. The version I learned growing up was described by Martin Luther (in the 1500s) as having an introduction, seven petitions, and a conclusion.

Our Father who art in heaven
Hallowed by Thy name.
Thy kingdom come.
Thy will be done on earth as it is in heaven.
Give us this day our daily bread.
And forgive our trespasses as we forgive
those who trespass against us.
And lead us not into temptation.
But deliver us from evil.
For thine is the kingdom and the power and
the glory forever and ever. Amen.

My mom had made choices for her life with the free will God gave her. At that point, she gave herself to God our Father, and his will be done. Matthew 26 and Luke 22 tell us that Jesus went to pray in a place called Gethsemane before he was about to be arrested and then crucified. He prayed to God our Father for a way out while submitting to "your will be done." As a human, how afraid and weary he must have been.

Then Jesus went with them to a place called
Gethsemane, and he said to his disciples, "Sit

here, while I go over there and pray." And taking with him Peter and the two sons of Zebedee, he began to be sorrowful and troubled. Then he said to them, "My soul is very sorrowful, even to death; remain here, and watch with me." And going a little farther he fell on his face and prayed, saying, "My Father, if it be possible, let this cup pass from me; nevertheless, not as I will, but as you will." And he came to the disciples and found them sleeping. And he said to Peter, "So, could you not watch with me one hour? Watch and pray that you may not enter into temptation. The spirit indeed is willing, but the flesh is weak." Again, for the second time, he went away and prayed, "My Father, if this cannot pass unless I drink it, your will be done." And again he came and found them sleeping, for their eyes were heavy. So, leaving them again, he went away and prayed for the third time, saying the same words again. Then he came to the disciples and said to them, "Sleep and take your rest later on. See, the hour is at hand, and the Son of Man is betrayed into the hands of sinners. Rise, let us be going; see, my betrayer is at hand." (Matthew 26:36–46)

113

Psalm 23 is one of the chapters of the Bible that's probably familiar to most people, even to those who don't believe in God. The thing I love about it is it's relevant, no matter what phase of life we're in. David wrote it so brilliantly simple and yet so succinct. It's a beautiful description that helps us visualize how our Lord provides for all our needs in our life on earth and in heaven.

My mom was "walking through the valley of the shadow of death." She couldn't physically walk, but she knew she was going to die very soon. She had no fear of dying. While she was experiencing physical pain and discomfort, her soul was clearly comforted.

Psalm 23 is applicable to all our days of living here on earth. Just as Jesus gave instruction that we don't need to heap up empty phrases in our prayers because our Father knows what we need before we ask him, we are also given simple instructions for how we should live our lives here on earth. God created us, gave us free will, and knows we are imperfect. And that is why he gave us Jesus.

Nate and I visited my mom after work the next day. It was so hard to go to work when I wanted to be with my mom instead, knowing I had little time left to spend with her. I didn't have any options for getting the time off of work and keep my job. My mom was supportive and understanding of my situation. And, fortunately, other family members and her loyal friend, Al, were able to visit her as well. None of us wanted her to be alone in her hospital room. And everyone who loved her was hoping to get the opportunity to visit with her one last time.

Although she was still bleeding, she was holding up pretty well, and we had a very nice visit. I can't imagine what it must feel like to have your loved ones visit you, knowing it's likely the last time they'll see you here on earth. Leaving her was more difficult than ever for me because although I didn't know if she'd survive until my next visit in the past, knowing there was nothing that could be done if and when she would start bleeding to death made it feel different.

I cherished every minute with her. I had so many unanswered questions for so many years, and throughout this time with her being sober, I was getting answers that I desperately needed for my own healing. I believe God knew that both my mom and I needed this time to heal our hearts and minds. My mom was back to giving of herself selflessly for her daughter. And she was teaching me about faith in God again. It's been thirty-two years, and my heart breaks as the tears flow as I write this. Alcohol had robbed my mom and I of a loving relationship for half of my life with her. And I felt loved by my mom again. Jesus was there for me. Jesus was there for my mom. Jesus is there for you. He loves us without fail.

The Lord is my shepherd; I shall not want.
He makes me lie down in green pastures.
He leads me beside still waters.
He restores my soul.
He leads me in paths of righteousness for his name's sake.

Even though I walk through the valley of the shadow of death,
I will fear no evil, for you are with me;
your rod and your staff, they comfort me.
You prepare a table before me in the presence of my enemies;
you anoint my head with oil;
my cup overflows.
Surely goodness and mercy shall follow me all the days of my life,
and I shall dwell in the house of the Lord forever.

—Psalm 23

114

The next two days were uneventful. No bleeding was detected. My mom was getting dehydrated easily, so she was given IVs on and off as they monitored her needs. When I visited her on the first of those two days, she was really cheerful and even ate some ice cream. She continued to think of things she wanted me to take care of when she was gone. Without alcohol, she always was conscientious. She even thought about returning some pickle jars to the woman who had made pickles for her. By that time, our many conversations about her dying and how she would like things done had become the norm and as ordinary as talking about the weather.

On the second of those two days, I didn't get to the hospital to visit her. I don't remember why and I didn't add those details to the notes I documented. I called her instead. One of my cousins (daughter of my godmother) who visited her often and my mom's friend, Al, were there. My mom was too tired and coughing too much to talk to me for long. I remember feeling bad when I couldn't be with her. And I felt so grateful for everyone who was making the drive to Rochester to visit with her because I didn't want her to feel alone. And many more people were praying for her. Clearly, she was loved very much.

God gave us a few days that were calm. It was as though he surrounded us all with protection from chaos and some time to rest our souls. Proverbs 30:5 tells us, "Every word of God proves true; he is a shield to those who take refuge in him."

And Psalm 18:30 tells us, "This God—his way is perfect; the word of the Lord proves true; he is a shield for all those who take refuge in him."

Again, different books of the Bible with the same message. I believe the words I read in the Bible. Jesus was there for me. He's there for all of us. I find refuge in him daily. I hope you can too.

Sometimes I pray in complete silence, no words, just feeling close to God, knowing he knows my heart and the words I need to say. I don't intend to do it. I pray long prayers with an evolving list of people I pray for by name. Sometimes I start praying, and without realizing it, my mind just goes blank and finds rest. When I realize it, sometimes I start my long prayer again and sometimes I just praise God and know that he knows what I was going to say already. I love the ability to pray in silence, just being quiet, feeling and trusting God, taking refuge from the busyness of life. I should do that more often.

"When you pass through the waters, I will be with you; and through the rivers, they shall not overwhelm you; when you walk through fire you shall not be burned, and the flame shall not consume you" (Isaiah 43:2).

115

On Thursday, September 20, 1990, my mom and I learned from her care team that we would need to find a nursing home for her to move to. I thought the message sounded rude and harsh because in essence, what they said was there was no need for her to take up a bed in the hospital when there was nothing they could do for her in terms of medical treatment. I don't remember being offered hospice care, and at that time, I didn't know anything about it. So I don't think I fully understood why we had to move my mom. Now I understand that no one knew how long she would live and it was time for her to move to comfort care.

It seemed like it made a big difference for my mom too. She looked white to me, like when someone "turns white" before passing out or when really ill. She was very quiet, not wanting to talk with me like we had been. And she had vomited from the medications they were giving her, so she decided to stop taking all of them, except morphine. So at that point, she was down to having morphine and the catheter that she was really irritated by at that point. But since she couldn't walk, it was necessary. The only good thing was there was still no bleeding detected.

So on that Friday, it was on me to try to find a nursing home with a room open to take her. My cousin (my godmother's daughter) who visited her often worked at a nursing home in Hudson. She provided care and sat with people who were dying there. My mom really wanted to go there, so her own niece would be there, and she'd be close by her sister's home. My mom found great comfort in knowing my cousin had experience with accompanying people while they died.

If you've never been responsible for arranging for a loved one's final wishes while they're alive, let me tell you that you want nothing more than to fulfill their wishes exactly how they would like. I felt so much pressure (self-induced). I was twenty-six years old and had no idea what I was doing. What were the chances that a room would be open with short notice?

Jesus was there for me. By the grace of God, they could arrange for a room for her at the nursing home where my mom wanted to go. I can't tell you how relieved I was. Then it was a matter of arranging for transportation for her to get from Rochester to Hudson. I was able to get everything coordinated for her to move on the following Monday. I didn't get much done at work that day, but my coworkers were very understanding and supportive. I made my usual phone calls to activate our network for updating everyone. But this time, I suggested that everyone who wanted to see her potentially for the last time should go to Rochester during the weekend.

After work, my brother and I went together to visit our mom. We were able to tell her the good news that she would be moving to where she wanted to go after the weekend. She was happy with that and was doing fairly well. "Doing fairly well" was all in perspective at that point. Seeing her in the condition she was in was a bit shocking to her loved ones who hadn't seen her since her health declined so badly. I felt so sorry for my mom. She was going through so much pain and suffering. My brother and I stayed as long as we could. We each gave our mom a big hug, told her we loved her, and reluctantly left to go home.

"Now may our Lord Jesus Christ himself, and God our Father, who loved us and gave us eternal comfort and good hope through grace, comfort your hearts and establish them in every good work and word" (2 Thessalonians 2:16–17).

116

Over the weekend, most of my mom's family visited her. I remember how amazing it felt to see my family members in the hospital, all of us hugging and sharing memories about how wonderful my mom was. The good memories are the ones that stay with me and the way I choose to remember my mom. Each of them took their turn for having alone time with my mom. Although it was exhausting for my mom, I think it brought her peace to have those last conversations, hugs, and opportunities to say, "I love you."

My mom started falling asleep off and on while her family members took their turns visiting. Many of them told me they just soaked in the quiet time and prayed for her while holding her hand. I'm so grateful that my mom and her family members were given that opportunity. Tears are pouring down as I go back to that day in my mind. I remember feeling like the heavy weight I had been carrying was lightened by being surrounded by the love of our family. The hallway and waiting room at the hospital was filled full with her loved ones. The hospital staff was very accommodating and even offered to bring coffee and water for us.

My mom was the youngest of the seven siblings, so her older brothers and sisters were having a really hard time trying to accept that their baby sister was dying. For some of them, it was quite shocking to see her in the condition she was in. Many of my cousins had stayed overnight at our house when we were younger, and a couple even lived with us for a while, one to provide day care for my brother and I and one to commute to work with my mom. My mom was a "favorite" aunt. She had clearly earned a very special place in the hearts of everyone who loved her.

By Sunday afternoon, my mom was starting to get confused easily. Her bloat was getting worse, and she was very tired. The doctor explained to me that her body was no longer able to get rid of the toxins that the liver normally filters out. So the toxins were getting to her brain, and we should expect for her brain function to decline further. She was sleeping most of the time. I thought we were losing her at that point.

The hospital staff thought it would be a while yet and strongly encouraged me to go home and get some rest. They assured me that they would take great care of her and get her ready for her trip to the Christian Community Home of Hudson the next day. As I had done many times before, I begged them to call me if anything changed overnight. I really didn't want her to be alone when she died.

After thirty-four days at Mayo Clinic Hospitals, I walked out for the last time. Only three of those days I hadn't made the trip there to be with my mom. I reflected on the past five weeks. My mom had gone through so much. We had no hope, then hope, then no hope. The care she was given there was phenomenal. We couldn't have asked for anything better. Many of the best physicians in the world had given her the best care possible.

Jesus was there for me. And he was there for my mom and everyone who loved her. That five-week period is one of the most pivotal in my life. After half of my life with my mom in the grip of alcoholism, I had five weeks with her sober. The healing I experienced by having the opportunity to talk with my mom and to truly feel loved by her again without having to separate her from her alcoholism changed the trajectory of the rest of my life. I really don't think I would have been able to become the person I am if I hadn't received that gift from God and from my mom.

"Thanks be to God for his inexpressible gift!" (2 Corinthians 9:15).

117

My mom made the trip to the Christian Community Home of Hudson. There are so many amazing people in the world who provide every kind of care, and I appreciate every single one of them. Thank God there are people with those very special gifts who are willing to use them to serve others. That's what God wants is for each of us to love and serve others using whatever gifts we're given, big or small.

There was no way to estimate the exact timing of my mom's arrival, so I had asked the care providers at the nursing home to call me when she arrived, and I would leave work to visit her in her new room. And, of course, I would have received a call if something had gone wrong. There was some uncertainty about whether or not moving her and riding in a medical van for over an hour could cause her to start bleeding badly.

With God's grace, she made it there without incident. When I arrived, she was resting in her new room. She seemed very peaceful. I sat quietly with her and held her hand. I didn't want to disturb nor wake her. Eventually, she woke up and looked at me. But her mind was really getting lost. I didn't know if she even knew what was going on. At that moment, I realized I had already had my last conversation with her. She couldn't speak coherently and seemed to be having trouble controlling movements. She seemed to be able to listen to me, but I'll never know how much of what I said was received. I had to hope the sound of my voice was comforting her. At least she made it back to Wisconsin. That's what she wanted. And I was able to help make that happen for her.

Jesus was there for me. As you can imagine, this was very difficult for me. Clearly, the time for her to go to her heavenly home with Jesus was near. That was my first experience being with someone who was dying. I prayed for her. As much as I didn't want to live the rest of my life here on earth without my mom, I tried to follow her lead to trust God and pray for "thy will be done."

She had suffered so horribly for so long, and I was given the gift of time with her to help me heal. I was so grateful for that, but I didn't want her to suffer anymore. During that time, since then, and especially while writing and sharing the pages of this book, people have shown their kindness and told me that I'm so strong. I may be, but not as strong as my mom. My strength comes from the Lord, and hers did too. She planted the seed of faith in me. She nurtured and helped me grow my faith. My faith became unshakable throughout the whole experience of her alcoholism.

While writing this book, I hadn't pulled out the things I saved from after my mom's passing. As I was nearing the last few days of her life in my story, I panicked a little, thinking that I wasn't sure how to end it. I pulled out the things I saved and read through everything. God put it clearly in my heart how it should end, based on the things I found. I continue to be humbled by how God works when I trust him.

One of the things I found melted my heart. I had saved her tax returns that I found from the years since she lost her job and got divorced from my dad. She lived on very little, less and less over those last six years. She had documented her annual bills. Over time, important things like health insurance were dropped because she couldn't afford them. There was no record of money donated to the church until 1989, the last full year she lived. She gave $29 to the church.

"For to set the mind on the flesh is death, but to set the mind on the Spirit is life and peace" (Romans 8:6).

118

The next day, a few of my mom's loved ones joined me to sit with her. We all knew the end was near. Nate; my brother, his wife, and son; and Mom's friend, Al, joined me there. My mom was actively dying. Every breath was a moan. She attempted to scratch an itch on her face, but when she'd try to raise her hand, it just fell back down. I gently scratched her itch for her. She couldn't say what she was trying to say and she couldn't really swallow anything. We all felt helpless, so mostly, we just sat quietly, holding her hand or saying what we needed to say to her.

She was getting great comfort care. The nurse that came on duty for the 3:00–11:00 shift was the sister of one of my best friends. I was so happy to see her and felt much more comfortable knowing someone I knew well was caring for my mom. We all stayed as long as we could. My brother said his final goodbye. Nate and I were the last to leave. My friend's sister promised she would call as soon as anything would change. She understood how much I wanted to be there for my mom but encouraged us to go home and get some rest. There was no way to tell how long my mom would remain the same.

Nate and I had both vehicles there, so we drove home separately. I cried the entire way home while talking to God. For the first time, I completely gave it all to God. I cried out. I begged him to please end my mom's suffering and take her to her heavenly home. It was late. I was exhausted from watching my mom suffer, and my heart was breaking for her. I remember the night sky seeming extra spectacular that night.

Nate and I had been home for less than an hour when my friend's sister called. She cried as she told me my mom was bleeding, and this was it. She was bleeding to death. I quickly called my godmother, and Nate and I sped off. The half hour drive felt like it took forever. I knew my godmother and cousin would get there quickly, but I just had to be there for my mom.

We rushed to my mom's room. My godmother and cousin were sitting at her side farthest from the door. My mom's eyes were closed as I walked toward her. I took her hand into mine as I sat down. She looked right into my eyes with her big beautiful blue eyes, and even though she couldn't speak, we were communicating. "I love you." Then her eyes closed again.

I looked at my cousin. I could see she was monitoring my mom's pulse on her wrist. She quietly told me that it was all but gone. My mom had waited for me to get there.

Although my mom hadn't been able to speak for almost three days, she looked up and said very clearly, "Okay." At that moment, I felt Jesus! My mom looked up again and said very clearly, "Okay." I felt Jesus there. He had come to invite her to go with him! There was a peace like I've never felt before or since. My mom looked up a third time and said very clearly, "Okay." And she passed. Jesus was there for me. He made his presence known as he welcomed my mom into heaven. There is nobody who could convince me otherwise.

On Wednesday, September 26, 1990, at 12:53 a.m., my mom went into the loving arms of Jesus. Her life on earth was forty-nine years, four months, and three days. My mom taught me a final and the biggest lesson in faith possible. It was in those final moments of her life that my faith became absolutely unshakable. I believe with all my heart and soul that Jesus was there. Even through all the trials of her alcoholism, my mom had kept her faith.

"I have fought the good fight, I have finished the race, I have kept the faith" (2 Timothy 4:7).

119

I sat there and held my mom's hand with both of my hands as I leaned my elbows on the bed. Nate, my godmother, and cousin left the room. I was trying to process what had just happened. It was the saddest moment of my life and at the same time the most amazing and beautiful moment. The pain and struggle was gone from my mom's face, and she looked so peaceful. There was no doubt in my mind she was made perfect, forgiven, redeemed, and celebrating a reunion with her loved ones who had gone before her. I wanted to spend a few more minutes in the room where I had felt Jesus come for my mom.

When I felt like I had soaked everything into my heart, there was one more promise. My mom had made me promise that I needed to be absolutely sure she was dead before she was cremated. So I sat and stared at her chest, and my imagination got the best of me. I had to keep this promise I had made. I stared and stared. I don't know how much time passed by. Nate came back in the room and gave me a hug as I sat there. He blocked my view, and in a panic, I pushed him away. So he had to talk some sense into me. He assured me that the nurse and eventually the funeral director would clearly confirm my mom's death. He helped me out of the room so I could call the funeral director we had chosen.

We all stayed until my mom's body had left the building. I had an appointment the next afternoon to plan my mom's funeral. My mom had shared with me all the things she wanted but also left some decisions for us. My brother was fine with whatever I wanted. I didn't give it much thought at the time, but nobody was able to break free from their jobs to join me for the meeting with the funeral director.

When I walked into his office, the funeral director welcomed me and said we would wait until the others arrived. I let him know that nobody else was coming. He was surprised but carried on with the tasks at hand. Then he paused, looked at me, and asked how old I was. I told him I was twenty-six. He looked at me with sincere sadness in his face and said, "I can't believe you're here alone." I told him I really didn't mind at all. And I wasn't alone. Jesus was there for me.

We accomplished all of the planning for her memorial service to be on Sunday, September 30. The songs and soloist were important to my mom. She had selected solos: "Abide with Me," "In the Garden," and "The Lord's Prayer." The song sung by the congregation was "I Know that My Redeemer Lives." How appropriate!

We selected Psalm 121 to be included in the memorial folder. When I found it again, I had written 116 ways Jesus was there for me throughout my journey with my alcoholic mom. Unsure of how to end my story, once again, God made it clear. I should trust him and end my story after 121 ways Jesus was there for me.

Psalm 121 is titled "My Help Comes from the Lord":

> I lift up my eyes to the hills. From where
> does my help come? My help comes from the
> LORD, who made heaven and earth. He will not

let your foot be moved; he who keeps you will not slumber. Behold, he who keeps Israel will neither slumber nor sleep. The LORD is your keeper; the LORD is your shade on your right hand. The sun shall not strike you by day, nor the moon by night. The LORD will keep you from all evil; he will keep your life. The LORD will keep your going out and your coming in from this time forth and forevermore.

120

My mom's funeral was well attended. She wanted it at her home church as a child. She had asked to be buried in the same plot as her dad and next to her mom. The pastor spoke about my mom's strong faith and trust in the Lord. I cried from the time I left home, through the service and her burial, and until I was talking with all our loved ones at the luncheon. Love never fails. The presence and kindness of everyone there filled me with love. Jesus was there for me and comforted me. The healing began. With God's grace, I had kept my promises to my mom. She had quit drinking, and I was there for her. And I received the gift of unshakable faith that has benefited me the rest of my life.

The next weeks and months were filled with all the usual things that need to be taken care of when someone dies. Cleaning out my mom's apartment was probably the hardest. I'm so happy I saved all the things that I did and didn't hastily throw away too much. I continued to attend Al-Anon meetings until I reached a point where I was comfortable with my healing and level of stress.

My mom's primary care doctor at Mayo mailed me a letter. It said:

> On behalf of the many physicians who cared for your mother during her recent hospital-

ization, may I express my deepest sympathies on your mother's passing. We all very much admired her courage in the face of the dreadful odds and regret that we were not able to resolve the problem. Please express our sympathies to other members of her family.

As we were ending the long journey with my mom, we sadly began another journey with Nate's sister falling into the grip of alcoholism. While I wasn't in the day-to-day interactions with my sister-in-law, we were involved often and could see her heading down the same path. My heart broke for her young boys, her parents, and her brothers. I thought to myself, *There's no way we're going to lose another loved one due to alcoholism.*

I thought maybe this was God's purpose for me having gone through everything I did with my mom. Maybe it was so I could make a difference and help Nate's sister overcome her alcoholism. I tried everything I could think of to try and said everything I could think of to say. Of course, everyone else who loved her did too. Over the years, the grip of alcohol grew tighter on her. We did what we could do to help her and help out her boys. Again, we were helplessly watching a loved one kill herself one drink at a time.

My sister-in-law's journey was the same as my mom's. Watching her parents and brothers trying to help her as much as I had tried to help my mom was heart-wrenching. She did work to be sober a couple of times but relapsed. Damn alcohol! Her journey lasted about the same amount of time as my mom's, and she died the same way. Only she died alone. None of us made it to the hospital in time to be with her. She was forty-two. Nate and I weren't even forty yet, and we had lost two beloved family members due to alcoholism and resulting cirrhosis and liver failure.

Our daughters were in grade school at the time. One had just finished the DARE program, and the other would start it the next year. Nate and I started talking with them about their risk for alcoholism. They're genetically predisposed to it from both sides of the family. My biggest fear is another person I love becoming an alcoholic, especially my own daughter. I truly do not think I can bear to helplessly watch another person I love die a slow, destructive, and painful death. I know Jesus is there for me, but I pray there's not a third for me. So far, so good.

"Whoever gives thought to the word will discover good, and blessed is he who trusts in the LORD" (Proverbs 16:20).

121

No matter how many years go by, I never stop missing my mom. And I'm sad that she's missed being here to watch her family grow. On the twenty-fifth anniversary of my mom's death, I got my life verse tattooed on my forearm: "Love never fails" (1 Corinthians 13:8). The same afternoon, I received a call from our older daughter. She was heading to the hospital for my first grandchild to be born. I was welcomed to join them and witnessed her birth the next day. She had a baby boy a year later. And our younger daughter had a baby boy five years later. I'm truly blessed.

I'm happy my mom has a grandbaby with her in heaven, due to my miscarriage, and I know they'll greet me when I arrive there someday. Jesus was there for me back when I was a teenager contemplating suicide. I had so much more life to live and God's purposes for me to fulfill. He's been there for me throughout the rest of my life. The main point I'd like you to take away is that Jesus is there for you. Like me, you have a loving Father God and Friend Jesus always there for you.

I don't know why I flirted with alcohol at all after my mom died. My brother hasn't. Drinking alcohol is so engrained in our culture. It's difficult to be the only one not drinking alcohol while with a group of people. Every time I'd give drinking a try, I'd start sliding into the grip of alcohol. Jesus was there for me. I'd realize I was at risk and stop drinking completely again. Although I've been sober for the majority of my life, I should have never flirted with alcohol as many times as I did.

For most of us who have watched someone fall into the grip of alcohol and not get out until death, we want his or her legacy to help save others. Throughout my writing, I grew a special bond with a woman I had known for a very long time but had no idea how similar our life stories are. We are sisters in Christ. We separately rose out of the darkness of deep pain and desperation from loving an alcoholic. We share unshakable faith and are proudly forever more sober. We share the same deep compassion for those who love alcoholics. And we love each other like sisters.

She introduced me to her niece who had lost her beloved dad to alcoholism. She, too, has incredible faith in God. His family members had gathered to be there for him as he was dying. My sister in Christ told me the Lord spoke to her and said, "Take that photo." The photo speaks a million and one words without a word printed. It was taken just days before he died. His bruised hands (caused by liver failure) each clinging to a beer can, one open and the other waiting to be opened. That's the power of alcoholism.

God provides for our needs and brought us with our stories together. When I asked, they gave me permission to use the photo for my book. I don't have a photo like that of my mom, but it would have looked the same. Seeing my mom's bruised hands clinging to beer cans is etched in my memory—same brand too. I was so blessed to get the precious time with her sober at the end.

Jesus is there for you always. Our Lord is near. Nothing can separate us from his love, and he gives us rest. No matter what happens in our lives, how much we sin, and no matter how imperfect we are, he loves us with unfailing love. He died for our sins so that we can be redeemed if we just believe and accept his unconditional gift of forgiveness and eternal life in heaven with him.

"In him we have redemption through his blood, the forgiveness of our trespasses, according to the riches of his grace" (Ephesians 1:7).

CONCLUSION

Well, there it is: 121 ways Jesus was there for me. I hope you have no doubt that Jesus is there for you. I want to say that I can't believe I just wrote my first book! But I can't say that. I do believe it, and all glory goes to God. I'm fifty-eight years old, and writing a book was never on my list of to-dos nor on my bucket list. God called me so strongly that I couldn't resist.

I trusted God to work through me and use my life experience, knowing I wasn't capable of writing a book. It took nine months. I had no idea what to expect and was surprised at the level of details I was able to recall. There were days and even weeks when it wouldn't be clear to me what to write, and I needed to trust God's timing. He gave me everything I needed.

Writing has brought me healing I didn't know I needed. The feedback has been overwhelming and brought me to tears. I've been introduced to wonderful people who suffer(ed) the same pain. And I learned that people I know have or had struggles with alcoholism that I didn't know about before. And others think my book will help others simply grow their faith, even if there are no struggles with alcohol.

Personal testimony is very powerful and reaches people in different ways. I'm so happy that God called me so strongly, and I pray this book will reach those whom it may help. I pray for everyone to know Jesus is there for them and gives them the hope and strength that can only come from him.

So perhaps this is God's purpose for me having gone through everything I did with my mom. For me to trust him and write this book. Or perhaps it's a step toward another purpose for me. My faith became unshakable throughout my mom's alcoholism—from beloved daughter to scapegoat, to separation, to caretaker, and back to beloved daughter. It wasn't the worst thing to ever happen to someone, but it's my story to share with hope and trust in God that it helps someone.

God has blessed me richly. I try very hard not to take for granted the goodness. I am not perfect, and my life isn't perfect. But it's perfectly imperfect. The gift of unshakable faith is what gets me through everything in life. There have been many more very difficult seasons in my life where I allowed myself to get completely stressed out again but not enough to cause another seizure, and it's mostly because I still struggle with my desire to control things. I would think I would have learned by now that it isn't possible. I learned at a young age that I have no control over other people. But I still want it. I am a sinner. The best way I know how to relieve stress is to trust God more fully. It's hard but always works when I realize it's what I need to do.

As I mentioned in the beginning, I once learned that our greatest pain can be transformed into our greatest purpose. If I didn't fully believe it before being called to write this book, I certainly believe it now. And I am so completely humbled by how God has worked through me day after day to start with a blank page and fill it with words I didn't have, but he did. God bless you always!

"For the gifts and the calling of God are irrevocable" (Romans 11:29).

Original sketch by the author – 1978

Thank you Jesus. Your love never fails.

We probably looked like a perfect happy family.
Inside our home, our family was torn apart.

Our wedding day – 1986

End-stage alcoholism

Clinging to beer cans when death is imminent

ABOUT THE AUTHOR

JoAnn Place is one of millions affected by alcoholism. By age twelve, her mom had fallen into the grip of alcoholism. Verbally abused and blamed by her mom for her drinking, tearing the family apart, she found herself in dark places, secretly not wanting to live while acting like nothing was wrong. She desperately tried to stop her mom from killing herself one drink at a time and flirted with the risk of alcoholism herself. Jesus was there for her and provided everything she needed. In him, she found the peace, strength, and hope she needed to continue on and choose not to be a victim.

While still a teenager, Jesus led her to the perfect young man with his own brokenness to be there for her too. Together they have built a beautiful, fruitful life, trusting Jesus for guidance through the good times and the bad. Originally, they thought they never wanted children, but Jesus led them to a change of mind. They're blessed with two beautiful daughters and three gorgeous grandchildren. Their family is everything to them.

Having never thought about writing a book, during the Easter church service in 2022, God called her so strongly to write about how Jesus was there for her that she couldn't resist. Personal testimony is powerful, so she trusted God, and day after day, the empty pages filled with words, using her life experience. She prays for everyone to know Jesus is there for them, too, and gives God all praise and glory.

Printed in the USA
CPSIA information can be obtained
at www.ICGtesting.com
CBHW021347061123
1659CB00001B/1